Network Threat Testing
EC-Council | Press

Volume 5 of 5 mapping to

E | CSA™

EC-Council | Certified Security
Analyst

Certification

COURSE TECHNOLOGY
CENGAGE Learning™

Australia • Brazil • Japan • Korea • Mexico • Singapore • Spain • United Kingdom • United States

COURSE TECHNOLOGY
CENGAGE Learning™

Network Threat Testing:
EC-Council | Press

Course Technology/Cengage Learning
Staff:

Vice President, Career and Professional
Editorial: Dave Garza

Director of Learning Solutions:
Matthew Kane

Executive Editor: Stephen Helba

Managing Editor: Marah Bellegarde

Editorial Assistant: Meghan Orvis

Vice President, Career and Professional
Marketing: Jennifer Ann Baker

Marketing Director: Deborah Yarnell

Marketing Manager: Erin Coffin

Marketing Coordinator: Shanna Gibbs

Production Director: Carolyn Miller

Production Manager: Andrew Crouth

Content Project Manager:
Brooke Greenhouse

Senior Art Director: Jack Pendleton

EC-Council:

President | EC-Council: Sanjay Bavisi

Sr. Director US | EC-Council:
Steven Graham

For product information and technology assistance, contact us at
Cengage Learning Customer & Sales Support, 1-800-354-9706

For permission to use material from this text or product,
submit all requests online at **www.cengage.com/permissions**.
Further permissions questions can be e-mailed to
permissionrequest@cengage.com

Library of Congress Control Number: 2010928727

ISBN-13: 978-1-4354-8370-5

ISBN-10: 1-4354-8370-7

Cengage Learning
5 Maxwell Drive
Clifton Park, NY 12065-2919
USA

Cengage Learning is a leading provider of customized learning solutions with office locations around the globe, including Singapore, the United Kingdom, Australia, Mexico, Brazil, and Japan. Locate your local office at: **international.cengage.com/region**

Cengage Learning products are represented in Canada by
Nelson Education, Ltd.

For more learning solutions, please visit our corporate website at **www.cengage.com**

Printed in the United States of America
1 2 3 4 5 6 7 13 12 11 10

Brief Table of Contents

Table of Contents

Hacking and electronic crimes sophistication has grown at an exponential rate in recent years. In fact, recent reports have indicated that cyber crime already surpasses the illegal drug trade! Unethical hackers better known as *black hats* are preying on information systems of government, corporate, public, and private networks and are constantly testing the security mechanisms of these organizations to the limit with the sole aim of exploiting it and profiting from the exercise. High profile crimes have proven that the traditional approach to computer security is simply not sufficient, even with the strongest perimeter, properly configured defense mechanisms like firewalls, intrusion detection, and prevention systems, strong end-to-end encryption standards, and anti-virus software. Hackers have proven their dedication and ability to systematically penetrate networks all over the world. In some cases *black hats* may be able to execute attacks so flawlessly that they can compromise a system, steal everything of value, and completely erase their tracks in less than 20 minutes!

The EC-Council Press is dedicated to stopping hackers in their tracks.

About EC-Council

The International Council of Electronic Commerce Consultants, better known as EC-Council was founded in late 2001 to address the need for well-educated and certified information security and e-business practitioners. EC-Council is a global, member-based organization comprised of industry and subject matter experts all working together to set the standards and raise the bar in information security certification and education.

EC-Council first developed the *Certified Ethical Hacker,* C|EH program. The goal of this program is to teach the methodologies, tools, and techniques used by hackers. Leveraging the collective knowledge from hundreds of subject matter experts, the C|EH program has rapidly gained popularity around the globe and is now delivered in over 70 countries by over 450 authorized training centers. Over 60,000 information security practitioners have been trained.

C|EH is the benchmark for many government entities and major corporations around the world. Shortly after C|EH was launched, EC-Council developed the *Certified Security Analyst,* E|CSA. The goal of the E|CSA program is to teach groundbreaking analysis methods that must be applied while conducting advanced penetration testing. E|CSA leads to the *Licensed Penetration Tester,* L|PT status. The *Computer Hacking Forensic Investigator,* C|HFI was formed with the same design methodologies above and has become a global standard in certification for computer forensics. EC-Council through its impervious network of professionals, and huge industry following has developed various other programs in information security and e-business. EC-Council Certifications are viewed as the essential certifications needed where standard configuration and security policy courses fall short. Providing a true, hands-on, tactical approach to security, individuals armed with the knowledge disseminated by EC-Council programs are securing networks around the world and beating the hackers at their own game.

About the EC-Council | Press

The EC-Council | Press was formed in late 2008 as a result of a cutting edge partnership between global information security certification leader, EC-Council and leading global academic publisher, Cengage Learning. This partnership marks a revolution in academic textbooks and courses of study in Information Security, Computer Forensics, Disaster Recovery, and End-User Security. By identifying the essential topics and content of EC-Council professional certification programs, and repurposing this world class content to fit academic programs, the EC-Council | Press was formed. The academic community is now able to incorporate this powerful cutting edge content into new and existing Information Security programs. By closing the gap between academic study and professional certification, students and instructors are able to leverage the power of rigorous academic focus and high demand industry certification. The EC-Council | Press is set to revolutionize global information security programs and ultimately create a new breed of practitioners capable of combating the growing epidemic of cybercrime and the rising threat of cyber-war.

Penetration Testing Series

The EC-Council | Press *Penetration Testing* series, preparing learners for E|CSA/LPT certification, is intended for those studying to become Network Server Administrators, Firewall Administrators, Security Testers, System Administrators and Risk Assessment professionals. This series covers a broad base of topics in advanced penetration testing and security analysis. The content of this program is designed to expose the learner to groundbreaking methodologies in conducting thorough security analysis, as well as advanced penetration testing techniques. Armed with the knowledge from the Penetration Testing series, learners will be able to perform the intensive assessments required to effectively identify and mitigate risks to the security of the organization's infrastructure. The series when used in its entirety helps prepare learners to take and succeed on the E|CSA, Certified Security Analyst certification exam.

Books in Series
* *Penetration Testing: Security Analysis*/1435483669
* *Penetration Testing: Procedures and Methodologies*/1435483677
* *Penetration Testing: Network and Perimeter Testing*/1435483685
* *Penetration Testing: Communication Media Testing*/1435483693
* *Penetration Testing: Network Threat Testing* /1435483707

Network Threat Testing

Network Threat Testing discusses penetration testing as it relates to denial of service, password cracking applications, databases, virus' and Trojans, and data leakage. Coverage also includes how to manage logs and checking file integrity.

Chapter Contents

Chapter 1, *Denial-of-Service Penetration Testing*, covers how to run various attacks including, SYN, IP Fragmentation, ping of death, smurf attacks as well as how to test a server's e-commerce gateway and how to test a network for DoS vulnerabilities. Chapter 2, *Password Cracking Penetration Testing*, discusses how to find legitimate user IDs, how to extract passwords from Windows and Linux system files, how to run dictionary and brute-force attacks and more. Chapter 3, *Application Penetration Testing*, includes coverage how to perform requirement and desing testing and web testing on applications. Chapter 4, *Database Penetration Testing*, explains how to scan default ports, identify instance names, test for Buffer Overflows in Extended Stored Procedures and how to check the status of TNS listener running on Oracle server. Chapter 5, *Virus and Trojan Detection*, describes the steps that need to be taken to detect virus and Trojans as well as the tools that are used to detect and eliminate malware. Chapter 6, *Log Management Penetration Testing*, discusses log files, log file management and how to perform penetration testing on an organization's log file management infrastructure. Chapter 7, *File Integrity Testing*, explains the nuances of checking file integrity. Chapter 8, *Data Leakage Penetration Testing*, explains how to perform data leakage penetration to protect confidential data from malicious users.

Chapter Features

Many features are included in each chapter and all are designed to enhance the learner's learning experience. Features include:

* *Objectives* begin each chapter and focus the learner on the most important concepts in the chapter.

* *Key Terms* are designed to familiarize the learner with terms that will be used within the chapter.

* *Chapter Summary*, at the end of each chapter, serves as a review of the key concepts covered in the chapter.

Student Resource Center

The Student Resource Center contains updates to content, useful links to the EC-Council Community site and the Information Security Community site. These sites may include blogs, discussions, updates on the latest news in Information Security and more! Access the Student Resource Center with the access code provided in your book. Instructions for logging onto the Student Resource Site are included with the access code. Visit *www.cengage.com/community/eccouncil* for a link to the Student Resource Center.

Additional Instructor Resources

Free to all instructors who adopt the *Network Threat Testing* book for their courses is a complete package of instructor resources. These resources are available from the Course Technology web site, *www.cengage.com/coursetechnology*, by going to the product page for this book in the online catalog, click on the Companion Site on the Faculty side; click on any of the Instructor Resources in the left navigation and login to access the files. Once you accept the license agreement, the selected files will be displayed.

Resources include:

- *Instructor Manual*: This manual includes course objectives and additional information to help your instruction.

- *ExamView Testbank*: This Windows-based testing software helps instructors design and administer tests and pre-tests. In addition to generating tests that can be printed and administered, this full-featured program has an online testing component that allows students to take tests at the computer and have their exams automatically graded.

- *PowerPoint Presentations*: This book comes with a set of Microsoft PowerPoint slides for each chapter. These slides are meant to be used as a teaching aid for classroom presentations, to be made available to students for chapter review, or to be printed for classroom distribution. Instructors are also at liberty to add their own slides.

- *Labs*: The nature of the content of this book does not lend itself to "hands-on" lab activities. The labs presented for this book include additional reading activities to enhance student knowledge base.

- *Assessment Activities*: Additional assessment opportunities including discussion questions, writing assignments, internet research activities, and homework assignments along with a final cumulative project.

- *Final Exam*: Provides a comprehensive assessment of *Network Threat Testing* content.

Cengage Learning Information Security Community Site

This site was created for learners and instructors to find out about the latest in information security news and technology.

Visit *community.cengage.com/infosec* to:

- Learn what's new in information security through live news feeds, videos and podcasts.

- Connect with your peers and security experts through blogs and forums.

- Browse our online catalog.

How to Become E|CSA Certified

EC-Council Certified Security Analyst (E|CSA) complements the Certified Ethical Hacker (C|EH) certification by exploring the analytical phase of ethical hacking. While C|EH exposes the learner to hacking tools and technologies, E|CSA takes it a step further by exploring how to analyze the outcome from these tools and technologies.

E|CSA is a relevant milestone towards achieving EC-Council's Licensed Penetration Tester (LPT), which also ingrains the learner in the business aspect of penetration testing. The LPT standardizes the knowledge base for penetration testing professionals by incorporating the best practices followed by experienced experts in the field. The LPT designation is achieved via an application/approval process. LPT is obtained by holding both the CEH and ECSA, then completing the application process for LPT found here at *http://www.eccouncil.org/lpt.htm*.

E|CSA Certification exams are available through Authorized Prometric Testing Centers. To finalize your certification after your training, you must:

1. Apply for and Purchase an exam voucher from the EC-Council Community Site at Cengage: *www.cengage.com/community/eccouncil*.

2. Once you have your Exam Voucher, visit *www.prometric.com* and schedule your exam.

3. Take and pass the E|CSA certification examination with a score of 70% or better.

About Our Other EC-Council | Press Products

Ethical Hacking and Countermeasures Series

The EC-Council | Press *Ethical Hacking and Countermeasures* series is intended for those studying to become security officers, auditors, security professionals, site administrators, and anyone who is concerned about or responsible for the integrity of the network infrastructure. The series includes a broad base of topics in offensive network security, ethical hacking, as well as network defense and countermeasures. The content of this series is designed to immerse the learner into an interactive environment where they will be shown how to scan, test, hack and secure information systems. A wide variety of tools, viruses, and malware is presented in these books, providing a complete understanding of the tactics and tools used by hackers. By gaining a thorough understanding of how hackers operate, ethical hackers are able to set up strong countermeasures and defensive systems to protect their organization's critical infrastructure and information. The series when used in its entirety helps prepare readers to take and succeed on the C|EH certification exam from EC-Council.

Books in Series
- *Ethical Hacking and Countermeasures: Attack Phases*/143548360X
- *Ethical Hacking and Countermeasures: Threats and Defense Mechanisms*/1435483618
- *Ethical Hacking and Countermeasures: Web Applications and Data Servers*/1435483626
- *Ethical Hacking and Countermeasures: Linux, Macintosh and Mobile Systems*/1435483642
- *Ethical Hacking and Countermeasures: Secure Network Infrastructures*/1435483650

Computer Forensics Series

The EC-Council | Press *Computer Forensics* series, preparing learners for C|HFI certification, is intended for those studying to become police investigators and other law enforcement personnel, defense and military personnel, e-business security professionals, systems administrators, legal professionals, banking, insurance and other professionals, government agencies, and IT managers. The content of this program is designed to expose the learner to the process of detecting attacks and collecting evidence in a forensically sound manner with the intent to report crime and prevent future attacks. Advanced techniques in computer investigation and analysis with interest in generating potential legal evidence are included. In full, this series prepares the learner to identify evidence in computer related crime and abuse cases as well as track the intrusive hacker's path through client system.

Books in Series
- *Computer Forensics: Investigation Procedures and Response*/1435483499
- *Computer Forensics: Investigating Hard Disks, File and Operating Systems*/1435483502
- *Computer Forensics: Investigating Data and Image Files*/1435483510
- *Computer Forensics: Investigating Network Intrusions and Cybercrime*/1435483529
- *Computer Forensics: Investigating Wireless Networks and Devices*/1435483537

Network Defense Series

The EC-Council | Press *Network Defense* series, preparing learners for E|NSA certification, is intended for those studying to become system administrators, network administrators and anyone who is interested in network security technologies. This series is designed to educate learners, from a vendor neutral standpoint, how to defend the networks they manage. This series covers the fundamental skills in evaluating internal and external threats to network security, design, and how to enforce network level security policies, and ultimately protect an organization's information. Covering a broad range of topics from secure network fundamentals, protocols & analysis, standards and policy, hardening infrastructure, to configuring IPS, IDS and firewalls, bastion host and honeypots, among many other topics, learners completing this series will have a full understanding of defensive measures taken to secure their organizations information. The series when used in its entirety helps prepare readers to take and succeed on the E|NSA, Network Security Administrator certification exam from EC-Council.

Books in Series
- *Network Defense: Fundamentals and Protocols*/1435483553
- *Network Defense: Security Policy and Threats*/1435483561
- *Network Defense: Perimeter Defense Mechanisms*/143548357X
- *Network Defense: Securing and Troubleshooting Network Operating Systems*/1435483588
- *Network Defense: Security and Vulnerability Assessment*/1435483596

Cyber Safety/1435483715

Cyber Safety is designed for anyone who is interested in learning computer networking and security basics. This product provides information cyber crime; security procedures; how to recognize security threats and attacks, incident response, and how to secure internet access. This book gives individuals the basic security literacy skills to begin high-end IT programs. The book also prepares readers to take and succeed on the Security|5 certification exam from EC-Council.

Wireless Safety/1435483766

Wireless Safety introduces the learner to the basics of wireless technologies and its practical adaptation. *Wireless|5* is tailored to cater to any individual's desire to learn more about wireless technology. It requires no pre-requisite knowledge and aims to educate the learner in simple applications of these technologies. Topics include wireless signal propagation, IEEE and ETSI Wireless Standards, WLANs and Operation, Wireless Protocols and Communication Languages, Wireless Devices, and Wireless Security Network. The book also prepares readers to take and succeed on the Wireless|5 certification exam from EC-Council.

Network Safety/1435483774

Network Safety provides the basic core knowledge on how infrastructure enables a working environment. Intended for those in an office environment and for the home user who wants to optimize resource utilization, share infrastructure and make the best of technology and the convenience it offers. Topics include foundations of networks, networking components, wireless networks, basic hardware components, the networking environment and connectivity as well as troubleshooting. The book also prepares readers to take and succeed on the Network|5 certification exam from EC-Council.

Disaster Recovery Series

The *Disaster Recovery Series* is designed to fortify virtualization technology knowledge of system administrators, systems engineers, enterprise system architects, and any IT professional who is concerned about the integrity of the their network infrastructure. Virtualization technology gives the advantage of additional flexibility as well as cost savings while deploying a disaster recovery solution. The series when used in its entirety helps prepare readers to take and succeed on the E|CDR and E|CVT, Disaster Recovery and Virtualization Technology certification exam from EC-Council. The EC-Council Certified Disaster Recovery and Virtualization Technology professional will have a better understanding of how to setup Disaster Recovery Plans using traditional and virtual technologies to ensure business continuity in the event of a disaster.

Books in Series
- *Disaster Recovery* /1435488709
- *Virtualization Security*/1435488695

Acknowledgements

Michael H. Goldner is the Chair of the School of Information Technology for ITT Technical Institute in Norfolk Virginia, and also teaches bachelor level courses in computer network and information security systems. Michael has served on and chaired ITT Educational Services Inc. National Curriculum Committee on Information Security. He received his Juris Doctorate from Stetson University College of Law, his undergraduate degree from Miami University and has been working over fifteen years in the area of Information Technology. He is an active member of the American Bar Association, and has served on that organization's Cyber Law committee. He is a member of IEEE, ACM and ISSA, and is the holder of a number of industrially recognized certifications including, CISSP, CEH, CHFI, CEI, MCT, MCSE/Security, Security +, Network + and A+. Michael recently completed the design and creation of a computer forensic program for ITT Technical Institute, and has worked closely with both EC-Council and Delmar/Cengage Learning in the creation of this EC-Council Press series.

Chapter 1

Denial-of-Service Penetration Testing

Objectives

After completing this chapter, you should be able to:

- Test a network for DoS vulnerabilities
- Enumerate and describe Web testing tools for DoS penetration testing
- Enumerate and describe Java testing tools for DoS penetration testing
- Test a server with heavy loads
- Run a SYN attack
- Run an IP fragmentation attack
- Run a ping of death attack
- Run a smurf attack
- Test a server's e-commerce gateway

Key Terms

Denial-of-service (DoS) attack   an attack performed by sending illegitimate SYN or ping requests that overwhelm the capacity of a system

Distributed denial-of-service (DDoS) attack   an attack in which the attacking computer hosts are often zombie computers with broadband connections to the Internet that have been compromised by viruses or Trojan horse programs that allow the perpetrator to remotely control the machine and direct the attack

Load testing   a test performed by putting an artificial load on a server or application to test its stability and performance

Ping of death   a DoS attack in which the attacker sends a malformed or malicious ping message to the target, causing a denial of service

Port flooding   an attack that sends a large number of TCP or UDP packets to a particular port, creating a denial of service to that port

Teardrop attack   a kind of attack that sends a large number of overlapping IP fragments to crash an operating system

Introduction to Denial-Of-Service Penetration Testing

The purpose of a *denial-of-service (DoS) attack* is to lower the performance of a Web site or to crash the Web site entirely. A DoS attack is performed by sending illegitimate SYN or ping requests that overwhelm the capacity of a network. Legitimate connection requests cannot be handled when this happens. Services running on the remote machines crash due to the specially crafted packets that are flooded over the network. In such cases, the network cannot differentiate between legitimate and illegitimate data traffic. Denial-of-service attacks are easy ways to bring down a server. The attacker does not need to have a great deal of knowledge to conduct them, making it essential to test for DoS vulnerabilities.

Distributed Denial-Of-Service Attack

In a *distributed denial-of-service (DDoS) attack,* the attacking computer hosts are often zombie computers with broadband connections to the Internet that have been compromised by viruses or Trojan horse programs that allow the perpetrator to remotely control the machine and direct the attack, often through a botnet/dosnet. With such slave or bot hosts, the services of even the largest and best-connected Web sites can be denied.

Conducting a Denial-Of-Service Penetration Test

Launching a DoS attack can have a negative impact on the business of an organization. Therefore, prior to verifying a vulnerability to a DoS attack by actually launching it, the penetration testing team should check with the client.

The result of the attack can lead to a loss of reputation along with economic losses. A successful DoS attack can disable computers and, subsequently, an entire network. An attack launched by a moderately configured system can crash PCs that are of high value.

The following steps should be followed when conducting a DoS penetration test:

1. Test heavy loads on the server.
2. Check for systems and devices vulnerable to DoS attacks.
3. Run a SYN attack on the server.
4. Run a port-flooding attack on the server.
5. Run an IP fragmentation attack on the server.
6. Run a ping of death attack.
7. Run a Teardrop attack.
8. Run a smurf (ping flooding or ICMP storm) attack.
9. Run an e-mail bomber on e-mail servers.
10. Flood the Web site forms and guestbook with bogus entries.
11. Place huge orders on e-commerce gateways and cancel before reaching the payment screen.

Step 1: Test Heavy Loads on the Server

Load testing is performed by putting an artificial load on a server or application to test its stability and performance. It involves the simulation of a real-time scenario. A Web server can be tested for load capacity using the following tools:

- *Web Application Stress (WAS) tool*: The WAS tool was designed to measure the stress on a Web application. It simulates the real-time scenario in which a large number of users make requests to a Web application. Web application developers use WAS to gauge their applications in extreme conditions. It can help the developer estimate the stability and performance of an application. WAS creates a real-time testing environment for Web applications.

- *JMeter*: JMeter is an open-source Web application load-testing tool developed by Apache. This tool is written entirely in Java. so it can be fully integrated with Java Web applications. JMeter is used to measure the performance and stability of a Web application.

- *TestLoad*: TestLoad is an automated load-testing tool for IBM iSeries servers. It is used to accomplish the following goals:
  - Imitate original system performance
  - Place an artificial load on the network
  - Monitor and capture server jobs and batch activity

Step 2: Check for Systems and Devices Vulnerable to DoS Attacks

The penetration tester should check the system for a DoS attack vulnerability by scanning the network. The following tools can be used to scan networks for vulnerabilities:

- *Nmap*: Nmap is a tool that can be used to find the state of ports, the services running on those ports, the operating systems, and any firewalls and filters. Nmap can be run from the command line or as a GUI application.
- *GFI LANguard*: GFI LANguard is a security-auditing tool that identifies vulnerabilities and suggests fixes for network vulnerabilities. GFI LANguard scans the network, based on the IP address/range of IP addresses specified, and alerts users about the vulnerabilities encountered on the target system.
- *Nessus*: Nessus is a popular open-source scanning tool that can determine the vulnerabilities in a system.

Step 3: Run a SYN Attack on the Server

A penetration tester should try to run a SYN attack on the main server. This is accomplished by bombarding the target with connection request packets. The following tools can be used to run SYN attacks:

- *Trinoo*: The Trinoo utility launches coordinated UDP flood denial-of-service attacks from many sources. It consists of a large number of servers, or masters, and a large number of clients, or daemons. An attacker using the Trinoo network connects to a Trinoo master and instructs the master to launch a denial-of-service attack against one or more IP addresses. The Trinoo master, in turn, communicates with the daemons, giving instructions to attack one or more IP addresses for a specified period.
- *Tribe Flood Network*: The Tribe Flood Network (TFN) is a distributed tool used to launch coordinated denial-of-service attacks from many sources against one or more targets. Apart from generating UDP flood attacks, a TFN network also generates TCP SYN floods, ICMP echo request floods, and ICMP directed broadcast denial-of-service attacks. TFN has the capability to generate packets with spoofed source IP addresses.
- *Synful*: The Synful tool can send SYN packets to particular ports and target IP addresses from spoofed source IP addresses and ports. The following command is used to execute this tool:

```
synful <target _ IP> <port> <number _ of _ times>
```

- *Synk4*: Synk4 is a DoS attack tool that mainly targets TCP/IP networks. The Synk4 tool can perform random IP spoofing by sending SYN messages to a specific range of ports. The following command is used to execute this tool:

```
synk4 <srcIP> <target _ IP> <low _ port> <high _ port>
```

Step 4: Run a Port-Flooding Attack on the Server

Port flooding sends a large number of TCP or UDP packets to a particular port, creating a denial of service on that port. The main purpose of this attack is to make the ports unusable and increase the CPU's usage to 100%. This attack can be carried out on both TCP and UPD ports.

The following tools can be used to conduct a port-flooding attack:

- *Mutilate*: Mutilate is mainly used to determine which ports on the target are open. This tool mainly targets TCP/IP networks. The following command is used to execute Mutilate:

```
mutilate <target _ IP> <port>
```

- *Pepsi5*: The Pepsi5 tool mainly targets UDP ports and sends a specifiable number and size of datagrams. This tool can run in the background and use a stealth option to mask the process name under which it runs.

Step 5: Run an IP Fragmentation Attack on the Server

Penetration testers can use an IP fragmentation attack to send a large number of packets to a system in order to increase the system's CPU utilization to 100%. This attack works in two ways. In the first method, the attacker generates a large number of packets and sends all these packets simultaneously to the target system in order to crash the system or network. In the second method, the attacker sends packets that are overlapped, often causing a denial of service in the receiver. The following tools can be used to perform an IP fragmentation attack:

- *Syndrop*: This tool exploits Microsoft's SYN sequence number bug. The following command can be used to execute this tool:

  ```
  syndrop <srcIP> <target_IP> [-s src_prt] [-t target_prt]
  [-n number_of_packets]
  ```

- *Jolt2*: Jolt2 uses either ICMP or UDP traffic. This tool allows the user to specify both the target port and IP address. If the user specifies the port, Jolt2 will send UDP traffic; otherwise, it will send ICMP traffic to the port. The following command is used to execute this tool:

  ```
  jolt2 -s <srcIP> -p <target_port> <target_IP>
  ```

Step 6: Run a Ping of Death Attack

Ping of death is a DoS attack in which the attacker sends a malformed or malicious ping message to the target, causing a denial of service. This attack is performed by intentionally sending an ICMP ping packet that is larger than 65,536 bytes, which is the maximum size for an IP packet. Many systems cannot handle packets of that size, so they crash.

Step 7: Run a Teardrop Attack

A ***Teardrop attack*** involves sending a large number of overlapping IP fragments to crash the operating system. The following tools can be used to perform a Teardrop attack:

- *WinNuke*: WinNuke (Figure 1-1) is a Windows DoS attack tool that exploits the out-of-band (OOB) bug to crash the target hosts. This tool attempts to crash the target system by sending more packets than it can handle, leading to a system crash.

- *Ssping*: Ssping sends a group of highly fragmented, overlapped ICMP data packets to crash the target system.

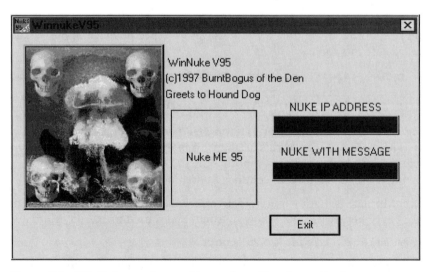

Figure 1-1   WinNuke can be used to perform Teardrop attacks.

Step 8: Run a Smurf (Ping Flooding or ICMP Storm) Attack

A smurf attack involves sending ICMP ping requests to broadcast addresses, with the source IP address of the request spoofed to be the IP address of the victim. When the victim receives the request, it responds, broadcasting the request to all hosts on the network, flooding the network with ICMP traffic.

Step 9: Run an E-Mail Bomber on E-Mail Servers

In this step, the penetration tester sends a large number of e-mails to test the target mail server. If the server is not protected or strong enough, it crashes. The tester uses various server tools that help send these bulk e-mails. The following tools are used to carry out this type of attack:

- *Mail Bomber*: Mail Bomber is a server tool used to send bulk e-mails by using subscription-based mailing lists. It is capable of holding a number of separate mailing lists based on subscriptions, e-mail messages, and SMTP servers for various recipients.
- *Attaché Email Bomber*: Attaché Email Bomber is a tool that allows a user to send a large number of messages with attachments. Its script can be easily modified.
- *Advanced Mail Bomber*: Advanced Mail Bomber is able to send personalized messages to a large number of subscribers on a Web site from predefined templates. The message delivery is very fast; it can handle up to 48 SMTP servers in 48 different threads. A mailing list contains boundless structured recipients, SMTP servers, messages, etc. This tool can also keep track of user feedback.

Step 10: Flood the Web Site Forms and Guestbook with Bogus Entries

In this step, the penetration tester fills online forms with arbitrary and lengthy entries. If an attacker sends a large number of such bogus and lengthy entries, the data server may not be able to handle it and may crash.

Step 11: Place Huge Orders on E-Commerce Gateways and Cancel Before Reaching the Payment Screen

A payment gateway is an electronic service used by e-commerce establishments to transfer money securely. Payment gateways provide an interface for credit card processing and other forms of electronic money transfers. This service encrypts confidential information such as credit card and bank account numbers so that the information is assured security during the transaction process.

The penetration tester should enter huge orders to test the application for various factors such as capacity, stability, performance, and robustness. If the application is well protected or strong enough to accept huge values, then an error message will be displayed. Otherwise, the application will crash. The tester should make a report of how the application responds to the various tests conducted on it.

Web Testing Tools

ISS Internet Scanner

The ISS Internet Scanner tool (Figure 1-2) scans the host's systems to determine if they are vulnerable to a variety of DoS conditions and attacks. This tool also provides background information on the attacks.

Mercury QuickTest Professional

Mercury QuickTest Professional offers a solution for functional test and regression test automation. Mercury QuickTest Professional implements the concept of keyword-driven testing to reduce the process of test creation and maintenance. This approach provides access to the core test and object properties by means of an incorporated scripting and debugging environment. QuickTest Professional is useful for both technical and non-technical users.

FlameThrower Stress-Testing Tool

FlameThrower is a validation solution for networks that provides network management solutions. It provides a way for advanced testing, independent of extensive scripting input. FlameThrower simulates numerous users accessing a site from numerous network segments. IDS solutions can be tested using FlameThrower by creating

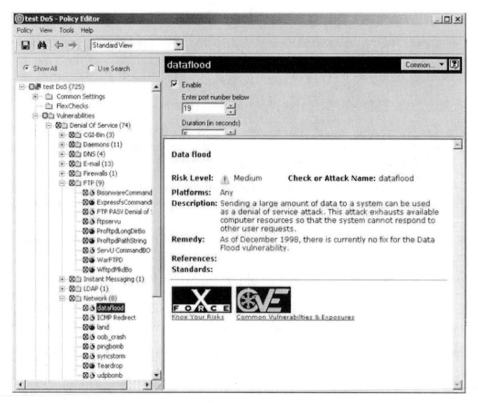

Figure 1-2   The ISS Internet Scanner can detect DoS vulnerabilities.

typical and nontypical user load situations with attack signature generators. FlameThrower integrates denial-of-service attack loads that can test the capabilities of IDS and firewall solutions.

Avalanche

Avalanche replicates user behavior and the application infrastructure. It overcomes the need for an expensive testing infrastructure by integrating the behavior of multiple users, up to 2 million, into a single device. Avalanche works in synchronization with Reflector test appliances to provide accurate multiple protocol responses to generated requests. The integrated systems test the capacity of any device or network connected between them.

Avalanche includes the following capabilities:

- Facilitates Web services testing and integrates multiple Web browsers and user behavior patterns
- Confirms protection against viruses and DDoS attacks
- Provides integrated statistics in a single report, and exports them into JPEG, PDF, or HTML formats

Avalanche Analyzer

Avalanche Analyzer (Figure 1-3) is a reporting tool that allows users to evaluate the data generated by the Avalanche testing tool. The data are represented in the form of graphs and reports. Avalanche Analyzer facilitates the analysis of multiprotocol tests by supporting protocols such as HTTP, SSL, and RTSP/RTP POP3. It employs the SNMP data for identifying the relationship between user response times detected by Avalanche and the performance of the user's network devices and servers. Avalanche Analyzer displays real-time statistics produced by Avalanche for critical variables across all protocols. Infrastructure can be determined while testing is in progress.

Pylot

Pylot (Figure 1-4) is used for testing the performance and scalability of Web services. This tool is useful for running HTTP load tests, which are used for capacity planning, benchmarking, analysis, and system tuning.

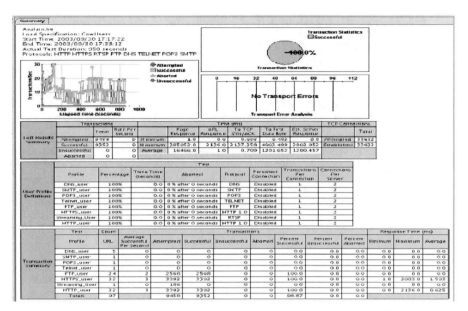

Figure 1-3   Avalanche Analyzer displays real-time statistics while testing is in progress.

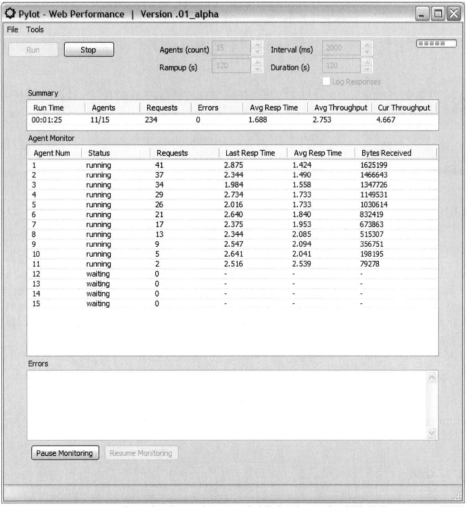

Figure 1-4   Pylot tests the performance and scalability of Web services.

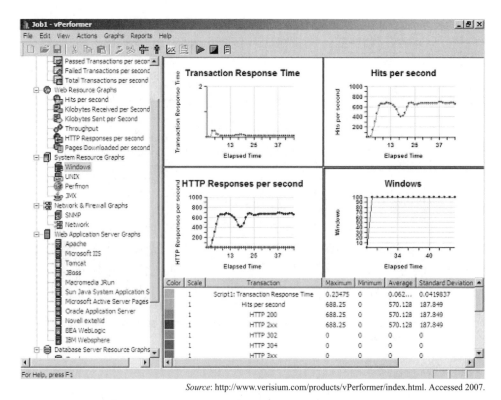

Figure 1-5   vPerformer assesses the performance and scalability of Web applications.

Pylot generates concurrent load (HTTP requests), verifies server responses, and produces reports with metrics. Test suites are executed and monitored from a graphical user interface (GUI).

Pylot includes the following features:

- Multithreaded load generator
- HTTP and HTTPS (SSL) support
- Execution/monitoring console
- Real-time statistics

vPerformer

vPerformer (Figure 1-5) assesses the performance and scalability of Web applications. This tool measures the performance characteristics of an application by generating automated test scripts. vPerformer enables the user to monitor the state of any associated external component that influences the behavior of an application. These components include Web servers, application servers, database servers, operating systems, network devices, and SNMP implementations.

vPerformer includes the following features:

- Does not a require a programming background
- Flexibility of distributed testing with a single point of control
- Support for multiple platforms, browsers, Web servers, application servers, and database servers over a LAN or WAN

Curl-Loader

Curl-Loader generates application load and behavior of thousands of HTTP/HTTPS and FTP/FTPS clients, each with its own IP address. This tool is useful for performance loading of various application services, testing Web and FTP servers, and generating traffic.

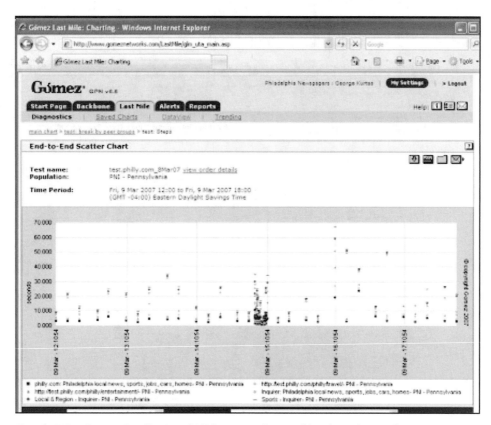

Figure 1-6 Gomez Reality Load XF is an on-demand load-testing tool.

Curl-Loader includes the following features:

- Supports HTTP 1.1. GET, POST, and PUT, including file upload operations
- Supports HTTP Web and Proxy Authentication (HTTP 401 and 407 responses) with Basic, Digest, and NTLM
- Full customization of client request HTTP/FTP headers
- URL fetching probability
- HTTP cookies and DNS caches
- Transfer limit rate for each client download or upload operation on a per-URL basis
- Connection establishment timers for each URL

Gomez Reality Load XF

Gomez Reality Load XF (Figure 1-6) is an on-demand load-testing tool that generates a real-world simulation of the actual traffic conditions produced by end users. External load tests minimize this risk and should be performed each time a new application is deployed, or whenever an important change or upgrade has been made to the operational infrastructure.

StressTester

StressTester (Figure 1-7) is an enterprise load- and performance-testing tool for Web applications. It monitors as many of the resources of the system under test as required. StressTester includes the following features:

- Zero scripting
- Suitable for any Web, JMS, IP, or SQL application
- Operating system independent

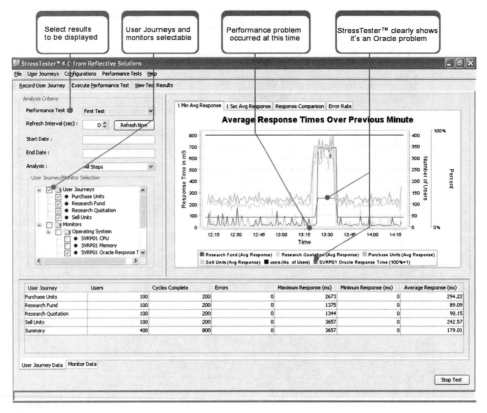

Figure 1-7 StressTester is an enterprise load- and performance-testing tool for Web applications.

The Grinder

The Grinder is a Java load-testing framework freely available under a BSD-style open-source license. It orchestrates activities of a test script in many processes across many machines, using a graphical console application. Test scripts make use of Java plug-ins. Most users do not write plug-ins themselves; instead, they use one of the supplied plug-ins. The Grinder comes with a mature plug-in for testing HTTP services, as well as a tool that allows HTTP scripts to be automatically recorded.

Proxy Sniffer

Proxy Sniffer is a Web load-testing and stress-testing tool. It includes the following capabilities:

- HTTP/S Web session recorder that can be used with any Web browser
- Automatic protection from false-positive results by examining actual Web page content
- Detailed error analysis using saved error snapshots and real-time statistics

FunkLoad

FunkLoad is a Web load-, stress-, and functional-testing tool written in Python and distributed as free software under the GNU GPL. FunkLoad emulates a Web browser (single-threaded), provides HTTPS support, and produces detailed reports in the ReST, HTML, and PDF formats.

Loadea

Loadea is a stress-testing tool that includes the following modules:

- *Capture module* provides a development environment and utilizes C# scripting and XML-based data.
- *Control module* defines, schedules, and deploys tests, defines number of virtual users, and more.
- *Analysis module* analyzes results and provides reporting capabilities.

LoadManager

LoadManager is a load-, stress-, stability-, and performance-testing tool from Alvicom. It runs on all platforms supported by Eclipse and Java, such as Linux and Windows.

TestLoad

TestLoad is an automated load-testing solution for IBM iSeries servers. Rather than placing an artificial load on the network, it runs natively on the server, simulating actual system performance and capturing batch activity, server jobs, and green-screen activity.

NeoLoad

NeoLoad is a load-testing tool for Web applications that allows users to design complex scenarios to handle real-world applications. NeoLoad includes the following features:

- Data replacement
- Data extraction
- System monitors
- SSL recording
- PDF and HTML reporting
- IP spoofing

PowerProxy

PowerProxy is a Windows-based HTTP/HTTPS proxy that has a range of basic load-testing features to test Web servers and show debugging information about every request and response received or sent.

HostedToolbox

HostedToolbox is a hosted load-testing service that features browser-based test script recording, with no downloads or system requirements. It works with any client or server, and is executed from a distributed infrastructure with servers in multiple locations.

Test Complete Enterprise

Test Complete Enterprise is an automated test tool with Web load-testing capabilities.

WebPartner Test and Performance Center

WebPartner Test and Performance Center is a test tool for stress tests, load performance testing, transaction diagnostics, and Web site monitoring of HTTP/HTTPS Web transactions and XML/SOAP/WSDL Web services.

QTest

QTest is a Web load-testing tool that supports all Web, Web service, J2EE, .NET, ASP, AJAX, CGI, and Mainframe Portal environments and, in particular, complex Web applications like Siebel, SAP, and Epiphany.
QTest includes the following features:

- Cookies managed natively
- HTML and XML parser
- Allows display and retrieval of any element from an HTML page or an XML flux in test scripts
- Option of developing custom monitors using supplied APIs

LoadDriver

LoadDriver is a load-testing tool that directly drives multiple instances of Internet Explorer, rather than simulating browsers. It supports browser-side scripts/objects, HTTP 1.0/1.1, HTTPS, cookies, cache, and Windows authentication. Tests can be scriptlessly parameterized with data from text files or custom ODBC data sources for the following parameters:

- Individual user ID and password
- Page to start
- Data to enter
- Links to click
- Initial cache state

SiteTester1

SiteTester1 is a load-testing tool. It allows users to define requests, jobs, procedures and tests, HTTP1.0/1.1-compatible requests, POST/GET methods, and cookies. It can be run in multithreaded or single-threaded mode. Reports are generated in HTML format, and the tool maintains and reads XML-formatted files for test definitions and test logs.

httperf

httperf is a Web server performance/benchmarking tool. It provides a flexible facility for generating various HTTP workloads and measuring server performance.

NetworkTester

NetworkTester passes real user traffic, including DNS, HTTP, FTP, NNTP, streaming media, POP3, SMTP, NFS, CIFS, and IM through access authentication systems such as PPPOE, DHCP, 802.1X, and IPSec, as necessary.

NetworkTester includes the following features:

- Unlimited scalability
- GUI-driven management station
- No scripting
- Open API
- Errors isolated and identified in real time
- Traffic monitored at every step in a protocol exchange (such as time of DNS lookup and time to log on to server)
- All transactions logged
- Detailed reporting

WAPT

WAPT is a Web load- and stress-testing tool with the following features:

- Handles dynamic content and HTTPS/SSL
- Support for redirects and all types of proxies
- Clear reports and graphs

Microsoft Application Center Test

Microsoft Application Center Test is a tool for stressing Web servers and analyzing performance and scalability problems with Web applications, including ASP, and the components they use. It supports several authentication schemes and the SSL protocol for use in testing personalized and secure sites. The programmable dynamic tests can also be used for functional testing.

ANTS Load

ANTS Load is a load- and stress-testing tool focused on .NET Web applications, including XML Web services. It generates multiple concurrent users via recordable Visual Basic .NET scripts and records the user experiences. At the same time, performance counter information from Windows systems is integrated into the results.

Apache JMeter

JMeter is a Java desktop application from the Apache Software Foundation designed to load-test functional behavior and measure performance. It can be used to test performance on static and dynamic resources (files, servlets, Perl scripts, Java objects, databases and queries, FTP servers, and more). JMeter can generate a graphical analysis of performance or test server/script/object behavior under heavy concurrent load.

TestMaker

TestMaker is a free open-source utility used for performance, scalability, and functional testing of Web applications. It includes the following features:

- XML-based scripting language
- Library of test objects to create test agents
- Capability to check and monitor e-mail systems using SMTP, POP3, and IMAP protocols

Siege

Siege is an open-source stress/regression test and benchmark utility that allows users to stress many URLs simultaneously. Siege includes the following features:

- Supports basic authentication, cookies, and HTTP and HTTPS protocols
- Enables testing a Web server with a configurable number of concurrent simulated users
- Stresses a single URL with a specified number of simulated users or stresses multiple URLs simultaneously
- Reports total number of transactions, elapsed time, bytes transferred, response time, transaction rate, concurrency, and server response

Web Polygraph

Web Polygraph is a benchmarking tool for caching proxies, origin server accelerators, L4/7 switches, and other Web intermediaries.

OpenSTA

Open System Testing Architecture is a free open-source Web load/stress-testing application licensed under the GNU GPL. It utilizes a distributed software architecture based on CORBA.

PureLoad

PureLoad is a Java-based multiplatform performance-testing and analysis tool that includes the following features:

- Dynamic input data
- Scenario editor/debugger
- Load generation for single or distributed sources

ApacheBench

ApacheBench is a Perl API for Apache benchmarking and regression testing. It is intended as a foundation for a complete benchmarking and regression-testing suite for transaction-based mod_perl sites. It can be used for stress-testing a server while verifying correct HTTP responses.

Torture

Torture is a simple Perl script for testing Web server speed and responsiveness, and the stability and reliability of a particular Web server.

eValid

eValid is a Web-testing tool that uses a test engine with the following functions:

- Browser-based client-side quality checking
- Dynamic testing
- Content validation
- Page performance tuning
- Web server loading
- Capacity analysis

WebSuite

WebSuite is a collection of load-testing, capture/playback, and related tools for performance testing of Web sites. WebSuite includes the following modules:

- Webcorder
- Load Director
- Report Generator
- Batch Manager

Forecast

Forecast is a load-testing tool for Web, client-server, network, and database systems. Forecast includes the following features:

- Proprietary, Java, or C++ scripting
- Windows browser or network recording/playback
- Network traces can also be taken from more than 15 third-party tracing tools
- Virtual user data can be parameterized
- Works with a wide variety of platforms

http-Load

http-Load is a free load-testing application that is used to generate Web server loads. It can handle both HTTP and HTTPS.

SilkPerformer

SilkPerformer is a load-testing tool that can simulate thousands of users working with multiple protocols and computing environments. It allows administrators to predict the behavior of e-business environments before an application is deployed, regardless of size and complexity.

LoadRunner

LoadRunner is a load-testing and stress-testing tool for Web applications and other types of applications. It supports a wide variety of application environments, platforms, and databases, and includes a large suite of network, application, and server monitors to enable performance measurement of each tier, server, and component, and the tracing of bottlenecks.

Java Test Tools

JavaCov

JavaCov is a J2SE/J2EE coverage-testing tool that specializes in testing to MC/DC (Modified Condition/Decision Coverage) depth. JavaCov includes the following features:

- Eclipse plug-in
- Report generation into HTML and XML

- Apache Ant integration
- Support for test automation

Jameleon

Jameleon is an open-source automated testing harness for acceptance-level and integration testing written in Java. This tool separates applications into features and allows those features to be tied together independently, in XML, creating self-documenting automated test cases. These test cases can then be data-driven and executed against different environments.

Agitator

Agitator is an automated Java unit-testing tool. It creates instances of classes being exercised, calling each method with selected dynamically created sets of input data and analyzing the results.

PMD

PMD is an open-source tool that scans Java code for potential bugs, dead code, duplicate code, etc. It works with a variety of configurable and modifiable rule sets and integrates with a wide variety of IDEs (integrated development environments).

Jlint

Jlint is an open-source static analysis tool that checks Java code and finds bugs, inconsistencies, and synchronization problems by performing data flow analysis.

Lint4j

Lint4j is a static Java source and byte code analyzer that detects locking and threading issues, as well as performance and scalability problems, and checks complex contracts, such as Java serialization, by performing type, data flow, and lock graph analysis.

FindBugs

FindBugs is an open-source static analysis tool used to inspect Java byte code for occurrences of bug patterns, such as difficult language features, misunderstood API methods, misunderstood invariants when code is modified during maintenance, simple mistakes such as typos, and use of the wrong boolean.

Checkstyle

Checkstyle is an open-source tool used for checking code layout issues, class design problems, duplicate code, and bug patterns.

Java Development Tools

AppPerfect Test Studio

AppPerfect Test Studio is a suite of testing, tuning, and monitoring products for Java development. It includes the following types of tools:

- Unit tester
- Code analyzer
- Java/J2EE profiler

QEngine

QEngine is a platform-independent test automation tool for Java application functionality, Java API, SOAP, regression, and Java application performance testing, as well as Web functionality and Web performance testing.

GJTester

GJTester is a Java unit, regression, and contract (black box) testing tool that enables test case and test script development without programming. This tool allows the user to test private and protected functions and server application modules without implementing test clients. It is useful for testing CORBA, RMI, and other server technologies as well.

qftestJUI

qftestJUI is a recording/playback test tool used for the creation, execution, and management of automated Java/ Swing application tests. It includes a natural user interface, scripting capabilities, and a component recognition algorithm that takes into account a variety of attributes. Recorded GUI elements, user actions, and associated data are automatically integrated into an editable tree view reflecting the hierarchical structure of the application's GUI.

Cactus

Cactus is a simple open-source framework for unit-testing server-side Java code (servlets, EJBs, tag libraries, filters, etc.). Its intent is to allow fine-grained continuous testing of all files making up an application through an in-container approach.

JUnitPerf

JUnitPerf allows performance testing to be dynamically added to existing JUnit tests. It enables quick composition of a performance test suite, which can then be run automatically and independent of other JUnit tests. It is intended for use when there are performance/scalability requirements that require rechecking while refactoring code.

Koalog Code Coverage

Koalog is a code coverage analyzer for Java applications. Its features include in-process or remote coverage computation, the capability of working directly on Java method binaries (no recompilation), predefined (XML, HTML, LaTex, CSV, text) or custom report generation, and session merging to allow for compilation of overall results for distinct executions.

Abbot Java GUI Test Framework

Abbot Java GUI Test Framework provides automated event generation and validation of Java GUI components, improving upon the very basic functions provided by the java.awt.Robot class. The framework may be invoked directly from Java code or accessed without programming through the use of scripts via Costello, a script editor/ recorder. It is suitable for use by both developers for unit tests and QA for functional testing.

Java Tool Suite from Man Machine Systems

This suite includes the following tools:

- *JStyle*: A Java source analyzer used to generate code comments and metrics such as inheritance depth, cyclomatic number, and Halstead measures
- *JPretty*: Reformats Java code according to specified options
- *JCover*: Test coverage analyzer
- *JVerify*: Java class/API testing tool that uses an invasive testing model, allowing access to the internals of Java objects from within a test script, and utilizes a proprietary OO scripting language
- *JMSAssert*: A tool for writing reliable software
- *JEvolve*: An intelligent Java code evolution analyzer that automatically analyzes multiple versions of a Java program and shows how various classes have evolved across versions
- *JSynTest*: A syntax-testing tool that automatically builds a Java-based test data generator

JProbe Suite

This suite is a collection of Java debugging tools that includes the following tools:

- *JProbe Profiler and JProbe Memory Debugger*: Used for finding performance bottlenecks and memory leaks
- *JProbe Coverage*: Code coverage tool
- *JProbe Threadalyzer*: Used for finding deadlocks, stalls, and race conditions

Krakatau Professional for Java

Krakatau is a software metrics tool that includes more than 7,000 procedural, complexity, and size metrics related to reusability, maintainability, testability, and clarity. It includes cyclomatic complexity, enhanced cyclomatic complexity, Halstead's software science metrics, LOC metrics, and MOOD metrics.

OptimizeIt

OptimizeIt is a profiler, thread debugger, and code coverage tool suite.

DevPartner Java Edition

DevPartner Java Edition is a debugging/productivity tool used to detect and diagnose Java bugs and memory and performance problems. It includes thread and event analysis as well as coverage analysis.

Chapter Summary

- The purpose of performing a DoS attack is to reduce the performance of a Web site or to crash the site.
- DoS and DDoS attacks are similar. The main difference is that DDoS is a distributed attack, wherein the attack is launched from various unsuspecting sources.
- A DoS attack can have a negative impact on the business of an organization.
- Attackers may try to flood a network, thereby blocking legitimate network traffic.
- Load testing is the process of putting an artificial load on a server or an application to test its stability and performance.
- A penetration tester should check a system for a DoS attack by scanning the network.
- Penetration testers should try to run SYN attacks on the main server.
- Ping of death is a DoS attack in which the attacker sends a malformed or malicious ping message to the target, causing a denial of service.

Chapter 2

Password Cracking Penetration Testing

Objectives

After completing this chapter, you should be able to:

- Find legitimate user IDs
- Extract passwords from Windows and Linux system files
- Create a profile to guess a password
- Build a dictionary list
- Run dictionary and brute-force attacks
- Break passwords with software tools
- Sniff clear text passwords

Key Terms

Brute-force attack   an attack that tries each set of possible groupings of every number, letter, and special character until a password is discovered

Dictionary attack   a password cracking attack that tries every word in a specific dictionary or word list to find an unknown password

Hybrid attack   an attack that tries to find a changed password by adding combinations of numbers and symbols to a previous password

Shoulder surfing   watching a user's keyboard or screen while he or she is logging in or entering confidential information

Social engineering   the process of obtaining desired information by manipulating people

Introduction to Password Cracking Penetration Testing

Passwords protect computer resources and files from unauthorized access by malicious users. Using passwords is the most effective way to protect information and to increase the security level of a company. Companies use a combination of passwords and user IDs to protect their resources from intrusions by hackers and thieves. Hackers use sophisticated tools to uncover the passwords of Web applications and exploit systems. They use various methods to gain access to a system, such as manual login attempts and dictionary-based attacks.

Some system software products use weak or no encryption to store and/or transmit their user IDs and passwords from the client to the server. This may lead to theft of data or use of computer resources by unauthorized users. One of the leading causes of network compromise is the use of easily guessable or decipherable passwords.

Password Cracking Techniques

Social Engineering

This technique is the easiest way to crack a password. In *social engineering*, attackers take advantage of people to gain personal information. The information can be items such as date of birth, name of pet, shopping habits, and so on. Hackers can use this information to guess passwords. A hacker may act as if he or she is calling from an important organization or from tech support and may ask for a password or other information. These types of attacks can be prevented through training and raising employee awareness. Trained users spot attacks and respond accordingly.

Shoulder Surfing

Shoulder surfing is simply watching either a user's keyboard or screen while he or she is logging in or entering confidential information. In this type of attack, the attacker must be near the user. This type of attack can be prevented by exercising caution when entering passwords. When entering a password, users should be aware of nearby onlookers and shield the keyboard from view.

Password Cracking Software

Nowadays, many password cracking tools are available that try a large number of different combinations of letters and numbers to crack passwords. Some password cracking software uses sophisticated algorithms to generate passwords, and other software attempts to crack passwords by examining the hashed password stored on disk or sniffed from the network.

Inference

Inference may seem like an ineffective method, but it can be a very effective means to hacking someone's password. Inference is the method of guessing the password of a user that an attacker has information about. The information could be date of birth, favorite TV show, a pet's name, or a phone number. The best way to avoid such attacks is to educate users. Administrators can require that users use strong and secure passwords that cannot be broken easily. They can make sure that passwords are a combination of letters, numbers, and special characters.

Use of Older Operating Systems

Hackers often exploit the use of older operating systems to bypass password authentication. Operating systems such as Windows 9x and Windows ME do not require passwords to log in. The only way to avoid these types of attacks is to switch to a more trusted and powerful operating system.

Types of Password Cracking Attacks

Dictionary Attack

A *dictionary attack* uses every word in a specific dictionary or word list to find an unknown password. In this attack, a large list of words is tried in rapid succession until the password is found. Many password cracking utilities use different dictionaries. Attackers can create their own dictionaries or download them from the Internet.

Brute-Force Attack

A *brute-force attack* can crack any password, but it takes time. It tries each set of possible groupings of every number, letter, and special character until the password is discovered. It can take time, depending on the password complexities and the speed of the computer.

Hybrid Attack

A *hybrid attack* tries to find a password by adding combinations of numbers and symbols to a previous password. When users change their passwords, they sometimes simply add some number to the end of their previous password. Such passwords are easy to crack and can be hacked easily. Thus, it is important to change the password completely rather than only changing it partially.

Steps in Password Cracking Penetration Testing

1. Obtain a valid user ID.
2. Extract /etc/passwd and /etc/shadow files from Linux systems.
3. Extract SAM file from Windows machines.
4. Identify the target person's personal profile.
5. Build a dictionary of word lists.
6. Brute-force passwords.
7. Use automated password crackers to break password-protected files.

Step 1: Obtain a Valid User ID

A valid user ID must be obtained before finding a password. Companies often use a variation of an employee's first name and last name to create user IDs. An example of the specific format used at the target organization can generally be found on the organization's Web site where contact information is listed. This format can then be applied to the targeted individual.

Obtaining a copy of the organization's internal telephone directory is another way to find user IDs. Vendors are often given generic user IDs and passwords to perform remote transactions. These types of user IDs and passwords generally have something to do with the software or project being worked on.

Step 2: Extract /etc/passwd and /etc/shadow Files from Linux Systems

There are many ways to store account information on a Linux system. It can be stored as a file that can only be read by the root user, or it can be stored in a one-way hash format. The password file for Linux is located in /etc and is a text file called passwd. By default, this file is readable by anyone on the system and could thus be a security vulnerability.

Shadow password format is another method for storing password or account information. The risk factor is less in shadow password format, as the file /etc/shadow is readable only by the root user, and it contains the actual encrypted passwords along with additional information about the account. The following features are added to the shadow password format:

- *Login defaults*: These are set in a configuration file (/etc/login.defs).
- Utilities for adding, modifying, and deleting user accounts and groups
- Password expiration and aging
- Account expiration and locking
- Control of user's password selection
- Dial-up passwords

Linux Password Example

```
nomad:HrLNrZ3VS3TF2:501:100:Simple Nomad:/home/nomad:/bin/bash
```

Linux passwords use the following fields:

- *Username*: This field contains the account's username. Usernames are case sensitive.
- *Password*: This is the one-way-encrypted password.
- *User ID*: This field contains a numerical user ID. User IDs are usually assigned by the adduser utility.
- *Group ID*: This is the primary group ID of the user.

- *User information*: This field is used to store any extra information about the user.
- *Home directory of user*: In this example, /home/nomad is the directory where the user's personal files and Web pages are stored.
- *Shell account of user*: In this example, this field is set to /bin/bash, which means the user defaults to using the bash shell.

Linux Shadow File Example

In Linux, the /etc/shadow file stores the real password in encrypted format for the user's account with added properties associated to the user's password. The example below shows the various fields in the /etc /shadow file:

```
Vivek: $1$fnffc$GteyHdicpGOfffXX40w#5:13064:0:99999:7
```

The following are the fields in this example:

- *Vivek*: Account username; typed in at the login prompt
- *1fnffc$GteyHdicpGOfffXX40w#5*: The encrypted password for this account
- *13064*: Last time the password was changed
- *0*: Minimum number of days required between password changes
- *99999*: Maximum number of days the password is valid
- *7*: The number of days the user is warned before the password expiration date

Step 3: Extract SAM File from Windows Machines

Windows 2000/XP passwords are stored in c:\winnt\system32\config\SAM. The following tools can be used to extract this file:

- SAMDUMP
- pwdump
- L0phtCrack

Extract Backup of SAM/Emergency Repair Disk

Sometimes, a Windows application stores passwords in a backup SAM file in the c:\winnt\repair directory. Some Windows applications store passwords in an emergency repair disk. Attackers can check both of these for duplicate root UID entries and use the pwdump and John the Ripper tools to extract the passwords from these files.

Check Registry

Many Windows applications store passwords in the registry file or on the hard drive as plaintext. Any attacker who has access to the registry files and who has some knowledge about the registry can easily get these passwords.

Check the Microsoft Server Message Block (SMB) Protocol

The Microsoft Server Message Block (SMB) protocol is used for file and print sharing. Attackers can run the NetBIOS Auditing Tool (NAT) and extract the passwords using the following command:

```
nat -u userlist.txt -p passlist.txt <IP _ address>
```

NAT can crack the password of the administrator by using a default list of passwords, as shown in Figure 2-1.

Check the Active Directory Database

Some Windows applications store the passwords in the Active Directory database files. These files are stored locally. Any person who has the access to these files can easily get the passwords.

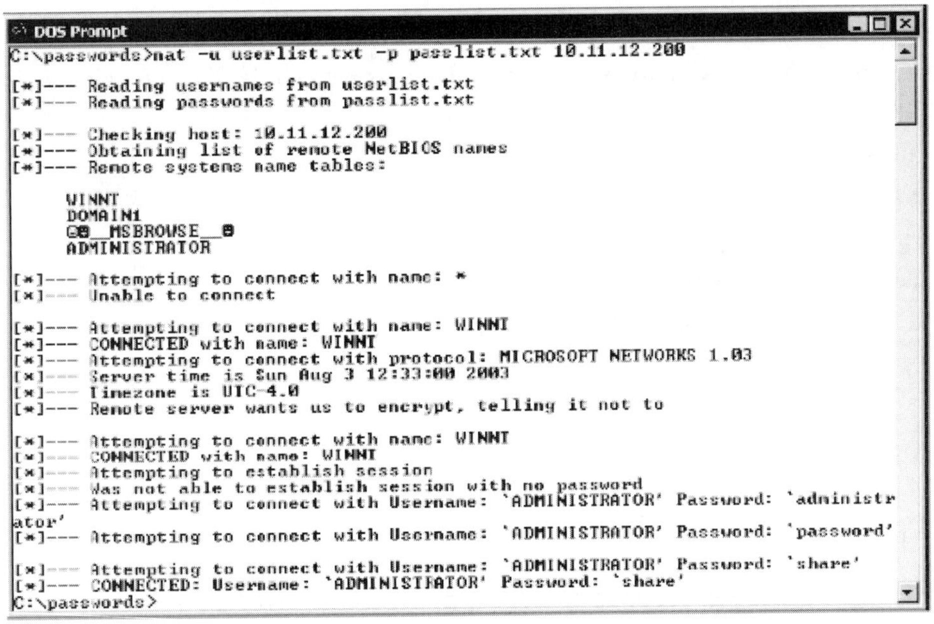

Figure 2-1   The NetBIOS Auditing Tool (NAT) can be used to extract passwords.

Step 4: Identify the Target Person's Personal Profile

Guessing an individual's password can be facilitated by creating a profile with information on that person. Personal information could include the following items:

- Telephone numbers
- Birthday, anniversary day, and special occasions
- Favorite movies, music, sports, books, and cartoon characters
- Education and interests
- Parents, relatives, and kids' names
- Project working on

All these pieces of information can be used to crack a password, because they are often used to create passwords. In light of this, the following parameters should be kept in mind while creating a password:

- Passwords should contain at least eight characters.
- Passwords should always be a combination of alphanumeric characters and symbols.
- Passwords should be changed at regular intervals.

Step 5: Build a Dictionary of Word Lists

Attackers can build a word list based on the information from the personal profile created in Step 4. Dictionary Maker is software that can be used to create a word list by extracting words from multiple source text files. Passlist is another example of this type of software.

Step 6: Brute-Force Passwords

Attackers can run dictionary and brute-force attacks to crack passwords. The following tools can be used to run these types of attacks:

- Brutus
- L0phtCrack
- Munga Bunga
- Password Cracker

Step 7: Use Automated Password Crackers to Break Password-Protected Files

Automated password cracking tools systematically guess passwords. The following tools can be used to crack passwords:

- Brutus
- Cerberus Internet Scanner
- CyberCop Scanner
- Inactive Account Scanner
- NetBIOS Auditing Tool (NAT)
- L0phtCrack
- John the Ripper
- SAMDUMP
- pwdump
- Webcrack

Extract Clear-Text Passwords from an Encrypted LM Hash

LM hashes contain clear-text passwords that are extracted from the end system's running window, as shown in Figure 2-2. Attackers can use the Cain & Abel tool to discover clear-text passwords from an encrypted LM hash.

Sniff Clear-Text Passwords from the Wire

Passwords can be sniffed from the wire by using tools such as dsniff. dsniff is a collection of tools for network auditing and penetration testing. dsniff, filesnarf, mailsnarf, msgsnarf, urlsnarf, and webspy passively monitor a network for interesting data (passwords, e-mail, files, etc.). arpspoof, dnsspoof, and macof facilitate the interception of network traffic normally unavailable to an attacker. sshmitm and webmitm implement active man-in-the-middle (MITM) attacks against redirected SSH and HTTPS sessions by exploiting weak bindings in ad hoc PKI.

Replay Attacks to Crack Passwords

Replay attacks are similar to MITM attacks. In these attacks, the packets sent to the server for authentication can be hacked with the help of monitoring tools. The communication can be changed or intercepted by the hacker so that next time the user will not get the chance to log into the system. Attackers use tools like Ethereal, Tcpdump, and WinDump, which are network analyzer or sniffer tools.

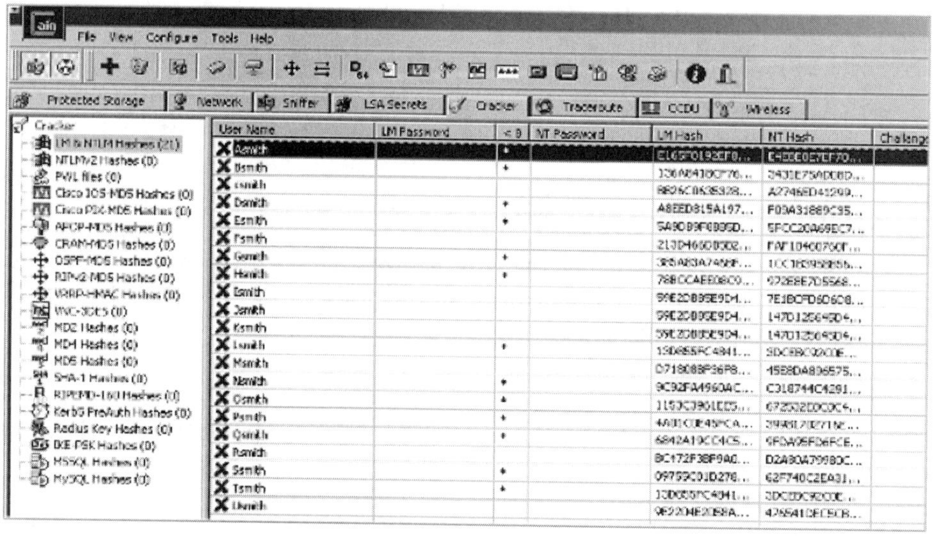

Figure 2-2 LM hashes contain clear-text passwords that can be extracted with the use of Cain & Abel.

Tools

SAMInside

This program (Figure 2-3) extracts Windows NT/2000/XP/2003 usernames and passwords. SAMInside includes six types of password attacks: brute-force attack, distributed attack, mask attack, dictionary attack, hybrid attack, and precalculated rainbow tables attack.

Dictionary Maker

Dictionary Maker (Figure 2-4) extracts all words from source text files and puts them into an output dictionary (word list) used for password recovery. Duplication of any keyword is eliminated in this tool.

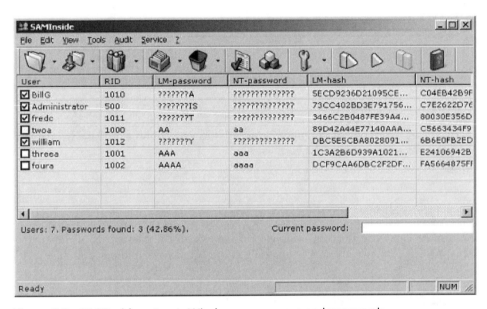

Figure 2-3   SAMInside extracts Windows usernames and passwords.

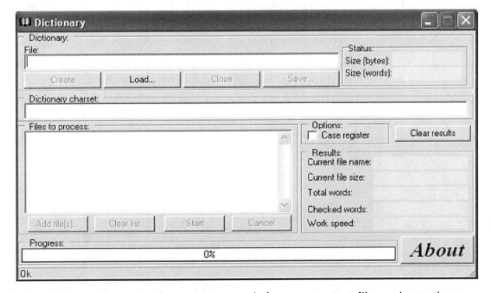

Figure 2-4   Dictionary Maker extracts words from source text files and puts them into an output word list for password recovery.

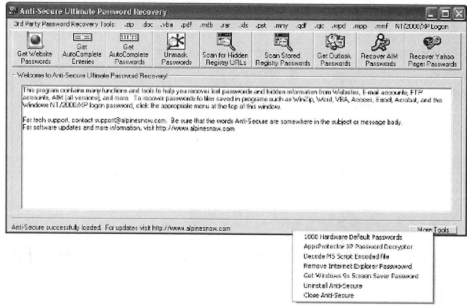

Figure 2-5 Anti-Secure Ultimate Password Recovery shows all the passwords in the current Windows user's password list file.

Anti-Secure Ultimate Password Recovery

Anti-Secure Ultimate Password Recovery (Figure 2-5) shows all the passwords in the current Windows user's password list (PWL) file. Password list files are kept in the Windows directory and have a .PWL extension.

Chapter Summary

- Passwords protect computer resources and files from unauthorized access. Companies use a combination of passwords and user IDs to protect their resources against intrusions by hackers and thieves.

- The password file for Linux is located in /etc and is a text file called passwd. By default, this file is readable by anyone on the system and could lead to a security vulnerability.

- One of the leading causes of network compromise is the use of easily guessable or decipherable passwords.

- A brute-force attack can crack any password, but it takes time. It tries each set of possible groupings of every number, letter, and special character until the password is discovered.

- Companies often use a variation of an employee's first name and last name to create user IDs.

- Guessing an individual's password can be facilitated by creating a profile with information on that person.

- Passwords can be sniffed from the wire by using tools such as dsniff.

Chapter 3

Application Penetration Testing

Objectives

After completing this chapter, you should be able to:

- Understand defects and failures
- Perform requirements and design testing
- Perform Web application testing
- Use Web application testing tools

Key Terms

Exception when an error occurs in a Java environment

Principle of least privilege the security concept that a user or system should only have the least amount of privilege to be able to perform the assigned task, and no more

Race condition a situation that occurs when various processes access and manipulate the same data at the same time, and the outcome of the process depends on the specific order in which the access takes place

Trap session a dummy session in a session fixation attack

Introduction to Application Penetration Testing

Application testing is an essential part of the software development process, helping to ensure error-free and reliable software. This includes both software application testing and Web application testing. Application testing involves meticulously testing every part of an application to check for vulnerabilities. This chapter teaches you how to carry out application penetration testing.

Defects

Programmers usually make at least a few mistakes when creating a program. These mistakes can potentially cause the programs to become dangerous. Defects come from mistakes in implementing product specifications. For example, the specifications may indicate that an application must contain a spell-check feature. If the final product does not contain the spell-check feature, that absence is considered to be a defect.

Defect identification costs are greater in the test and usage phases. To reduce development costs and time, developers should focus on preventing or eliminating defects before starting the testing process. This can be difficult; on average, leading software developers produce software with about one defect for every 30,000 lines of source code.

Defects Versus Failures

Testing is critical for any product's success. A penetration tester tests the software to track down any defects. A defect becomes a failure if it causes an error in the program's operation or negatively impacts a user's experience. Not all defects turn into failures, but at the same time, a single failure may ruin the usefulness of an entire application.

Requirements and Design Testing

Penetration testers should ask the following questions when performing requirements and design testing:

- Which users can access the program?
- Are there different user classes?
- Does each user class have the correct privileges?
- Can a user of one class obtain additional privileges?

Web Application Penetration Testing

Web applications are generally a collection of scripts residing on a Web server and interacting with databases or other sources of dynamic content. These applications are useful for collecting, processing, and broadcasting information over the Internet. Programmers protect this data in several ways, such as formatting the data elements in the HTTP requests using protocols that encode and hide the data elements. They also use Web application environments such as ASP and PHP, which pass data on to the developer without allowing intruders to track that data. Penetration testing identifies any issues with input validation and security.

To perform penetration testing on Web applications, testers should follow the steps in the following sections.

Step 1: Fingerprint the Web Application Environment

First, testers need to identify the Web application environment. They should gather information such as the scripting language and Web server software in use, as well as the operating system of the target server.

Step 2: Investigate the Output from HEAD and OPTIONS HTTP Requests

The header of any page returned from a HEAD or OPTIONS request will usually contain a SERVER: string detailing the Web server software version, and possibly the scripting environment or operating system in use. The following is an example header returned from an OPTIONS request:

```
OPTIONS / HTTP/1.0
HTTP/1.1 200 OK
Server: Microsoft-IIS/5.0
Date: Wed, 04 Jun 2003 11:02:45 GMT
MS-Author-Via: DAV
Content-Length: 0
Accept-Ranges: none
DASL: <DAV:sql>
DAV: 1, 2
Public: OPTIONS, TRACE, GET, HEAD, DELETE, PUT, POST, COPY, MOVE, MKCOL,
PROPFIND, PROPPATCH, LOCK, UNLOCK, SEARCH
Allow: OPTIONS, TRACE, GET, HEAD, COPY, PROPFIND, SEARCH, LOCK, UNLOCK
Cache-Control: private
```

Step 3: Investigate the Format and Wording of Error Pages

Some application environments, such as ColdFusion, have easily recognizable error pages. These pages, such as the 404 Not Found error page, will often give away the software version of the scripting language in use.

Step 4: Test for Recognized File Types, Extensions, or Directories

Different Web servers respond differently to file requests, depending on if the servers recognize the file extensions or not. Common file extensions such as .ASP, .HTM, .PHP, and .EXE should be tested during penetration testing. Testers should watch for any unusual output or error codes.

Step 5: Examine the Source of Available Pages

The source code from the openly accessible Web pages of the application front-end may provide clues as to the underlying application environment. The following is an example of the source code from a Web page that provides hints as to its environment:

```
<title>Home Page</title>
<meta content="Microsoft Visual Studio 7.0" name="GENERATOR">
<meta content="C#" name="CODE _ LANGUAGE">
<meta content="JavaScript" name="vs _ defaultClientScript">
```

Step 6: Manipulate Inputs in Order to Cause a Scripting Error

In this step, testers inject commands directly into a URL to try to force a scripting error. For example, Figure 3-1 shows a penetration tester manipulating the *ItemID* variable.

Step 7: Test the Inner Workings of the Web Application

There are many client-side programming scripts, such as JavaScript and VBScript, that provide a number of clues as to the inner workings of a Web application. For instance, consider the following code:

```
<INPUT TYPE="SUBMIT" on Click="
if (document. forms['product'].elements['quantity'].value >= 255) {
document.forms['product'].elements['quantity'].value='';
alert('Invalid quantity');
return false;
} else {
return true;
}
">
```

The maximum value of a *tinyint* field in most database systems is 255. From the previous code, it is clear that the targeted application is trying to keep the form handler safe from values that are larger than 255. This narrows down the possibilities of which system may be in use.

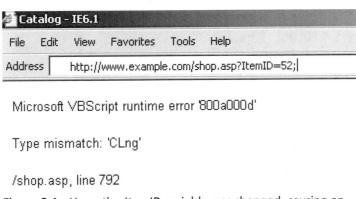

Figure 3-1 Here, the *ItemID* variable was changed, causing an error and revealing the scripting environment.

Step 8: Test Database Connectivity

Applications may require access to servers such as database servers. As with any other system, access rights should be limited to the minimum rights required, and these rights should be limited to only the duration necessary to perform the user's task. This conforms to the ***principle of least privilege***, which is the security concept that a user or system should only have the least amount of privilege to be able to perform the assigned task, and no more. Testers should check to make sure a target application does not have unrestricted administrator access rights.

Step 9: Test the Application Code

Penetration testers should check for the following in the application code:

- *Backdoors*: Developers may build backdoors into a program to facilitate debugging and troubleshooting. These backdoors provide a high level of access to the application and should be closed before they are used for malicious purposes.

- *Exception handling and failure notification*: When an error occurs during program execution in a Java environment, it causes an ***exception***. Testers should check how these are handled. These error messages can give information such as server names and root directories.

- *Login IDs and passwords*: Testers should check the comments in HTML code for hard-coded login IDs and passwords. These comments may also contain code paths, directory file names, or other file names.

Random Numbers Versus Unique Numbers

Testers should check for random numbers and unique numbers in the application code. Sometimes, developers use random numbers instead of unique numbers. These two concepts have the following differences:

- A random number can be any number within a certain range of numbers.

- A unique number is a number that will not repeat itself elsewhere in the code.

Random numbers may not always be unique numbers; the same number may appear more than once. It is necessary to check for random numbers and unique numbers in the application code, because attackers can predict the sequence of random numbers and use that knowledge to induce a software failure.

Figure 3-2 shows a random number generator.

Step 10: Test the Use of GET and POST

When a user clicks on a link in a Web page to go to an external site, the browser sends the URL of the source site to the destination site as the *REFERRER* variable. *GET* and *POST* variables are used as a part of the two-way conversation between the user and the network. Sensitive information is leaked in GET requests, because the user's input is directly shown in the URL.

POST commands, on the other hand, use the HTTP body to handle information. When a *POST* variable is used, the user's input can only be found by reading the source code of form-input pages. This means that the user's input is not as clearly displayed when using POST, so it is always advisable to use the *POST* variable instead of the *GET* variable in any Web application.

The following is an example of an HTTP request in a Web application:

```
GET /sample.php?var=value&var2=value2 HTTP/1.1
| HTTP-METHOD REQUEST-URI
PROTOCOL/VERSION
Session-ID: 361873127da673c
| Session-ID Header
Host: www.webserver.com
| Host Header
<CR><LF><CR><LF>|
Two carriage return line feeds
```

Figure 3-3 shows the result of a POST request.

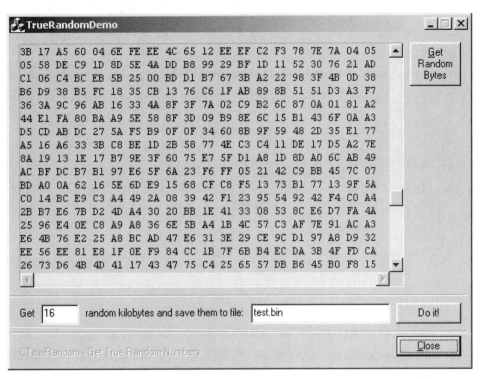

Figure 3-2   Random numbers may appear more than once in a program, while unique numbers appear exactly once.

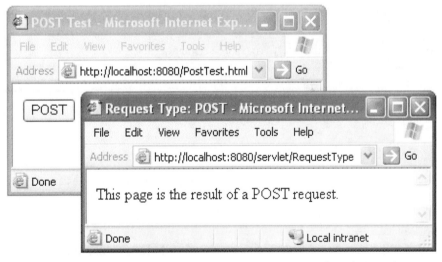

Figure 3-3   A POST request does not put the user's input directly into the URL, so it is more secure than a GET request.

Step 11: Test for Parameter-Tampering Attacks

Testers can alter parameter name-and-value pairs in a URL query string to attempt to retrieve sensitive information. For example, suppose *www.xsecure.com/bank_acctool.pdf* provides bank account information to an authenticated user. Testers can try changing the URL to *www.xsecure.com/bank_acct002.pdf*. If this pulls up the information for another account, the attack was successful.

As another example, consider a Web page that allows an authenticated user to select an account and debit the account with a fixed unit amount. When the user presses the **Submit** button, the application requests the following URL:

http://www.mydomain.com/example.asp?accountnumber=12345&debitamount=1

An attacker may change the URL parameters (*accountnumber* and *debitamount*) in order to debit another account, as follows:

http://www.mydomain.com/example.asp?accountnumber=67891&debitamount=9999

Step 12: Test for URL Manipulation

Testers should examine whether a server will deliver different Web pages by manipulating the URL. In a dynamic Web site, parameters are passed via the URL, such as the following:

```
http://targetsite/forum/?cat=2
```

```
Testers can try modifying the URL, such as:
```

```
http://targetsite/forum/?cat=6
```

If this loads a protected area, the site is not secure.

Step 13: Test for Cross-Site Scripting (XSS)

Testers should follow these steps to check for the Web application's vulnerability to cross-site scripting (XSS) attacks:

1. Inject code by breaking out the <h1> tag as follows:

```
http://www.targetsite.com/page.asp?pageid=10&lang=en&title=Section
%20Title</h1><script>alert('XSS%20attack')</script>
```

2. Use the TamperIE tool to intercept the client's GET and POST requests and retrieve the client-side JavaScript input validation code.

The following tools can help to test cross-site scripting:
- Paros Proxy
- Fiddler
- Burp Proxy
- TamperIE

Step 14: Test for Hidden Fields

Hidden fields in HTML source code sometimes carry sensitive data. Testers can check for hidden fields by implementing the following steps:

1. Try to view the page's source code by clicking the right mouse button on the Web page and selecting the **View Source** option.
2. Search for the string "hidden." This will show you hidden fields, like the following:

```
<input name="id" value="1234" type="hidden">
```

3. Save the page.
4. Remove the "type = hidden" text from the code.
5. Save the page.
6. Now, directly modify the field from the browser.
7. Click on the **Next** or **Send** button on the page.

Step 15: Test Cookie Attacks

Cookies store sensitive information that allows applications to:
- Authenticate the user's identity
- Speed up transactions

```
Example.c

    #include <stdio.h>
        int main(int argc, char **argv) {
            char small [4] = "SSS";
            char big [8] = "BBBBBBB";

            strcpy (big, "XXXXXXXX");
            printf ("%s\n", small);
        return 0; }
```

Figure 3-4   This script may cause a buffer overflow, which can make an application behave unexpectedly.

- Monitor behavior
- Personalize content

Testers should try manipulating local cookies to gain unauthorized access to the application.

Step 16: Test for Buffer Overflows

Sending too much data to a program may cause it to behave in an unexpected manner, and attackers can possibly use this technique to gain control of the host. Figure 3-4 shows an example of a script that might cause a buffer overflow.

Step 17: Test for Bad Data

Testers should try entering data that will cause an application to behave abnormally. For example, entering **</body></html>** into an application as a person's name may break pages that contain this name.

Step 18: Test Client-Side Scripting

Client-side scripting is one way that attackers can gain access to private information without valid credentials. To test for this type of attack, penetration testers can follow these steps:

1. Capture the URL after a valid logon.
2. Launch a new browser window and use the captured URL to go to the page that supposedly requires proper authentication.

If the supposedly secure page opens, the client-side scripting attack was successful.

Step 19: Test for Known Vulnerabilities

Web applications usually use third-party software, and many pieces of third-party software contain vulnerabilities. Testers can use a Web service such as Bugtraq to monitor these vulnerabilities.

Step 20: Test for Race Conditions

A *race condition* is a situation that occurs when various processes access and manipulate the same data at the same time, and the outcome of the process depends on the specific order in which the access takes place. Applications can use multiple threads to process multiple tasks at once. For example, a logon script may execute several server commands at once. An attacker may take advantage of this to interrupt the process and gain escalated privileges. Testers can check for race conditions in applications. Figure 3-5 shows an example of multiple threads.

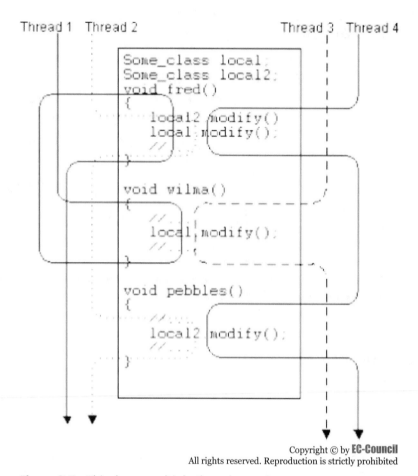

Figure 3-5 This shows multiple threads running at once.

Step 21: Test User Protection via Browser Settings

Web browsers have various security and privacy settings to protect users from harmful content. Testers should check to see how various settings will affect the application. For example, if cookies are disabled, what will the application do? If there is more than one Web browser installed in the system, testers can use a browser synchronization tool such as Sync2It, shown in Figure 3-6.

Step 22: Test for Command Execution Vulnerability

If a Web application does not properly filter user input, that input could trick the application into executing operating system commands. This will run the commands with the same permissions as the component that executed the command.

Perl allows for the piping of data from a process into an open statement by appending a | (pipe) character onto the end of a filename. For example, the following command executes /bin/ls and pipes the output to the open statement:

```
Open (FILE, "/bin/ls|")
```

Suppose that the original URL of a Web application is the following:

http://www.somedomain.com/cgi-bin/showInfo.pl?name=nason&template=tmp1.txt

The attacker can trick the Web application into executing the command **/bin/ls** by changing the template parameter value as follows:

http://www.somedomain.com/cgi-bin/showInfo.pl?name=nason&template=/bin/ls|

Many scripting languages allow programmers to carry out operating system commands during runtime by using various exec functions. An attacker can run arbitrary code if the application does not filter user input

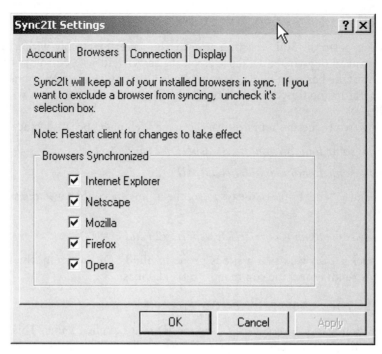

Figure 3-6   Sync2It synchronizes the security settings of multiple Web browsers on a single system.

for invalid entries. For example, the following is part of a PHP script that presents the contents of the system directory on UNIX systems:

```
exec("ls -la $dir",$lines,$rc);
```

By appending a semicolon (;) followed by an operating system command, it is possible to force a Web application into executing a command as follows:

http://www.somedomain.com/directory.php?dir=%3Bcat%20/etc/passwd

The result will retrieve the contents of the /etc/passwd file.

Step 23: Test for SQL Injection Attacks

Structured Query Language (SQL) is a programming language that accesses databases through queries. If a Web site constructs SQL statements from user-supplied input, attackers can exploit these sites by inserting code into that input, executing code on the server.

For example, a Web-based authentication form might have code like the following:

```
SQLQuery = "SELECT Username FROM Users WHERE Username = '" &
strUsername & "'AND Password = '" & strPassword & "'" strAuthCheck
= GetQueryResult(SQLQuersy)
```

In this code, the developer is taking the user's input from the form and embedding it directly into an SQL query. Suppose an attacker submits the following as the login and password:

```
Login: ' OR ''='
Password: ' OR ''='
```

This will cause the resulting SQL query to become:

```
SELECT Username FROM Users WHERE Username = '' OR ''='' AND
Password = '' OR ''=''
```

This will return a true result, and the attacker will then be logged in as the first user in the Users table.

Step 24: Test for Blind SQL Injection

When an attacker performs SQL injection attacks, the server may reply with a syntax error message. In blind SQL injection, instead of giving a database error, the server returns a customer-friendly error page and informs the user that a mistake has been made. This may mean that SQL injection is possible, but it may be difficult to detect. The general method used to identify blind SQL injection is to give a wrong and right statement in the parameter value.

The following two requests should return the same Web page, because "and 1=1" is always true:

- *http://www.somedomain.com/article.asp?ID=2+and+1=1*
- *http://www.somedomain.com/article.asp?ID=2*

However, because "and 1=0" is always false, the following could cause the site to return a friendly error, or no page at all:

- *http://www.somedomain.com/article.asp?ID=2+and+1=0*

Once the attacker discovers that a site is prone to blind SQL injection, this vulnerability can be easily exploited by simply sending specific commands to the database.

Step 25: Test for Session Fixation Attack

The session fixation attack forces a user's session ID to an explicit value. This can be done with a variety of techniques, including XSS attacks or using previously made HTTP requests. Once the user's session ID is fixed, the attacker waits for the user to log in, and then the attacker uses the predefined session ID value to assume the user's online identity.

There are two types of session management systems:

1. *Permissive systems* allow Web browsers to specify any ID.
2. *Strict systems* only accept server-side generated values.

With permissive systems, arbitrary session IDs are preserved without contact with the Web site. Strict systems need the attacker to preserve the session with periodic Web site contact to avoid inactivity timeouts.

Many Web sites use cookies for session IDs, but they may use URLs or hidden form fields as well. Most of the identified attack methods are directed toward cookies.

The session fixation attack is a three-step process:

1. *Session setup*: The attacker establishes a **trap session** (a dummy session used in a session fixation attack) for the target Web site and gains that session's ID.
2. *Session fixation*: The attacker forces the trap-session value into the user's browser as the user's session ID.
3. *Session entrance*: When the user logs into the target Web site, the fixed session ID value is used and the attacker takes over.

Fixing a user's session ID value can be achieved with the following techniques:

- Providing a new cookie value with a client-side script, exploiting a cross-site vulnerability
- Providing a cookie with the META tag, useful when the application will not allow XSS attacks in HTML script
- Providing a cookie with an HTTP response header, forcing any Web site in the domain to give a session ID cookie

Step 26: Test for Session Hijacking

The following are the steps for hijacking a session:

1. Locate a target user, find the user's active session, and track it.
2. Guess the sequence number (blind hijacking) of the data packets being sent back and forth between the session participants.
3. Check whether decommissioning the host causes a denial of service (DoS).
4. Hijack the session by sending data with the correctly guessed sequence number to the target recipient.
5. Resume the session after finishing the hijack to capture confidential data.

The following tools can be used for session hijacking:

- Juggernaut
- Hunt
- TTY-Watcher
- T-Sight

Step 27: Test for XPath Injection Attack

This attack technique can be used to exploit Web sites that construct XPath queries from user-supplied input. XPath is a language that can be directly used in an XML document or can be injected in an operation such as:

- XSLT transformation to XML document
- XQuery to XML document

The syntax of XPath is similar to that of an SQL query.

For example, suppose an XML document contains an element called *user*. Each of these has three subelements: *name*, *password*, and *account*. The XPath expression given below gives the account number of "Ivan," whose password is "Demo1234":

```
string(//user[name/text()=' Ivan ' and
password/text()='Demo1234']/account/text())
```

When an application makes use of a runtime XPath query construction, it may insert insecure user input into the query. If this is the case, it is easy for an attacker to inject malicious data into the query.

Suppose an application makes use of a runtime XPath query constructor that queries an XML document and tries to recover the account number of a user whose name and password are received from the client. Those applications may embed these values directly in the XPath query, as follows:

```
XmlDocument XmlDoc = new XmlDocument();
XmlDoc.Load("...");
XPathNavigator nav = XmlDoc.CreateNavigator();
XPathExpression expr =
nav.Compile("string(//user[name/text()='"+TextBox1.Text+"'
and password/text()='"+TextBox2.Text+
"']/account/text())");
String account=Convert.ToString(nav.Evaluate(expr));
if (account=="") {
// name+password pair is not found in the XML document
-
// login failed.
} else {
// account found -> Login succeeded.
// Proceed into the application.
```

When such code is used, an attacker can inject XPath expressions by providing the following value as the username:

```
' or 1=1 or ''='
```

This makes the query into the following:

```
string(//user[name/text()='' or 1=1 or ''='' and
password/text()='foobar']/account/text())
```

Because this will always be true, it is equivalent to the following:

```
string(//user/account/text())
```

Thus, this query will always return the first instance of *//user/account/text()*. The attack results in having the attacker logged in as the first user listed in the XML document, even though the attacker did not provide a valid username or password.

Step 28: Test for Server-Side Include Injection Attack

A server-side include (SSI) injection attack allows an attacker to send code to a Web application to be executed locally by the Web server. This takes advantage of a Web application's failure to check and sanitize user-supplied data before it is given to the server-side interpreted HTML file.

From the following SSI tag, the attacker can access the root directory on a UNIX-based system:

```
<!--#exec cmd="/bin/ls /" -->
```

The following SSI tag can allow an attacker to obtain database connection strings or other sensitive data contained within a .NET configuration file:

```
<!--#INCLUDE VIRTUAL="/web.config"-->
```

The following steps are used to secure SSI files:

1. Enable the suexec utility.
2. SSI-enabled files should have extensions other than .html or .htm, because these extensions pose greater security risks in a shared server environment. Extensions like .shtml can be used.
3. Servers can be disabled from running scripts and programs from SSI files. This can be done by using *IncludesNOEXEC* instead of *Includes* in the server's options.

Step 29: Test for Logic Flaws

A logic flaw is a failure in a Web application's logic to correctly perform conditional branching. This is difficult to catch using black-box testing. The best way to find logic flaws is to carefully audit the code. Consider the following example of PHP code:

```
<?php
$a=false;
$b=true;
$c=false;
if ($b && $c || $a && $c || $b)
echo "True";
else echo "False";
?>
```

The logic flaw in the above code is that if *$b* is true, the *if* statement will be completed successfully. This is not the intended outcome. It can be patched up with either of the following *if* statements:

```
if ($b && $c || $a && ($c || $b))
if ($b && $c || $a && $c || $a && $b)
```

Step 30: Test for Binary Attacks

Some of the most common binary attacks are format string bugs and buffer overflow attacks. Languages like C/C++ use static buffers, which makes them vulnerable to these attacks. A format string attack occurs when certain C functions, such as *printf(), fprint(), sprintf(), syslog(),* and *setproctitle(),* process special formatting characters (beginning with %).

Buffer overflow attacks occur when the amount of data stored is greater than the memory allotted. This causes the extra bytes to overflow into the adjacent locations in memory and overwrite the data in these locations. A buffer overflow attack may permit the attacker to control and disrupt the normal flow of execution. Compiled programming languages like C/C++ are more vulnerable to buffer overflow attacks than interpreted languages, including Java, Perl, PHP, and Python.

Buffer overflow attacks can be detected through black-box testing techniques.

Step 31: Test the XML Structure

The following are the steps to test the XML structure:

1. Send a large or malformed XML message to the server.

2. Check whether that message causes a denial of service (DoS).

3. Check all the parameters being validated, including:

- *enumeration*
- *fractionDigits*
- *length*
- *maxExclusive*
- *maxInclusive*
- *maxLength*
- *minExclusive*
- *minInclusive*
- *minLength*
- *pattern*
- *totalDigits*
- *whitespace*

Step 32: Test for XML Content-Level

An XML content-level attack involves creating an XML document containing malicious code in order to exploit the target system. The following are the steps to test for XML content-level:

1. Test the Web Service Definition Language (WSDL) with the WebScarab tool.

2. Modify the parameter's data based on the WSDL's definition for the parameter.

3. Check whether the Web service can be used with escalated privileges.

Step 33: Test for WS HTTP GET Parameters and REST Attacks

The following are the steps to test the WS HTTP GET parameters and REST attacks:

1. Examine the HTTP GET query string, for example:

    `https://www.ec.com/accountinfo?accountnumber=1234567&userId=aci9485jfuhe92`

2. Check the result of the string, for example:

    ```
    <?xml version="1.0" encoding="ISO-8859-1"?> <Account="1234567">
    <balance>€100</balance> <body>Bank of ECC account info</body>
    </Account>
    ```

3. Test the string for another vector (an entry point to attack), such as:

    ```
    "https://www.ec.com/accountinfo?accountnumber=1234567'
    exec master..xp _ cmdshell 'net
    user Vxr pass /Add &userId=asi9485jfuhe92"
    ```

4. Check the following:

- Maximum length and minimum length
- Validate payload
- Implement "exact match," "known good," and "known bad" in order
- Validate parameter names and existence

Step 34: Test for Malicious SOAP Attachments

1. Search for Web Service Definition Language (WSDL), which accepts attachments.
2. Attach and post a SOAP message with a nondestructive virus like EICAR.
3. Set parameter "true" in SOAP response with the UploadFileResult, which varies on each service.
4. Store EICAR test virus file on the host's server, and redistribute it as a PDF.

Step 35: Test for WS Replay

1. Install WebScarab and use it as a proxy to capture HTTP traffic.

2. Using the packets captured by Ethereal, use TCPReplay to initiate the replay attack by reposting the packet.

3. Resend the original message or change the message to determine the host server.

4. Capture many packets over time to determine session ID patterns in order to assume a valid session ID for the replay attack.

Application-Testing Tools

AtStake WebProxy

A proxy server acts as a mediator between a client and the server. It accepts requests made by the client and transfers them to the server, and then accepts the server response and passes it on to the client. Sometimes, the client request and the server response are modified.

Like any other proxy server, a Web proxy connects the client browser and the Web application. It captures and decodes the user's requests and provides the decoded requests to the server, and then furnishes the user with the required response generated by the server.

AtStake WebProxy is a scripted, automated testing tool used in black-box testing that helps in locating the vulnerabilities of Web applications.

SPIKE Proxy

SPIKE Proxy is an open-source Web application auditing tool. Its security features include the following:

- Multithreaded design
- Man-in-the-middle SSL proxying
- Form rewriting

SPIKE Proxy serves as an HTTP and HTTPS proxy. It also provides various automated tools used to identify vulnerabilities, including:

- Automated SQL injection
- Web site crawling
- Login from brute force
- Buffer overflow
- Directory traversal

The SPIKE Proxy tool enables the system administrator or the user to manipulate various components, such as cookies and headers, by penetrating Web applications and observing variables. The tool maintains a database of all requests made and replies sent, enabling the user to search and replace the requests if needed.

WebServerFP

The WebServerFP tool uses multiple HTTP requests, both malformed and valid, to determine the type of Web server it is currently testing. The responses are checked for two things:

1. HTTP code

2. The order of the items inside the header

KSES

KSES is a tool that filters HTML/XHTML in PHP. It rejects all unnecessary HTML attributes and checks the others for cross-site scripting (XSS), buffer overflows, and denial-of-service attacks.

Mieliekoek.pl

Mieliekoek.pl is an SQL inspection crawler. Its input is the output of the Web-mirroring tool HTTrack. It scans all forms in a Web site for SQL insertion problems. If it encounters these problems, it performs a simple SQL insertion and reviews the output. It can also do other tests, including tests for buffer overflow attacks.

Sleuth

Sleuth is a Web application assessment and analysis tool. It includes several plug-ins, such as:

- auxForms
- cmdLine
- testInputs
- charEncoding

While a normal proxy accepts a client's request, downloads the complete file, and then transfers it to the server, Sleuth's intercept proxy asynchronously transfers the request to the server even while it is still receiving the request.

WebGoat

WebGoat is a J2EE (Java 2 Enterprise Edition) Web security education tool. It is written in Java, and installers are available for both UNIX- and Windows-based systems.

WebGoat is an interactive learning environment, where the user locates a real vulnerability in each "class." The system on which users experiment is programmed to direct the learner with clues and guidelines while working.

AppScan

AppScan is a Web application security testing tool that merges well-developed security algorithms with scanning and reporting. Its main features include the following:

- Code sanitation
- Offline analysis
- Dashboarding

AppScan is a centralized server-based system that monitors testing, access permissions, reporting, and scanning rights.

URLScan

URLScan is a plug-in for IIS that permits only a certain set of HTTP requests. Enabling specific filters prevents malicious requests from attacking the server, including both known and unknown vulnerabilities.

Chapter Summary

- Software testing is an important part of the software development process.
- Web application penetration testing involves testing the following:
  - Environment
  - Database connectivity
  - Application code
  - Hidden fields
  - Cookie attacks
  - Buffer overflows
  - Bad data
  - Client-side scripting

- Race conditions
- Known vulnerabilities
- Command execution vulnerabilities
- SQL injection
- Blind SQL attacks
- Session fixation
- XPath injection attacks
- Logic flaws
- Binary attacks

Chapter 4

Database Penetration Testing

Objectives

After completing this chapter, you should be able to:

- Scan for default ports used by databases
- Identify the instance names used by databases
- Attempt to brute-force password hashes from the database
- Test for Buffer Overflows in Extended Stored Procedures
- Check the status of TNS listener running on the Oracle server
- Break into accounts using a dictionary attack

Key Terms

Brute-forcing the process of trying every possible password combination until one of them works

Database penetration testing the technique of testing a database for vulnerabilities to hacking attacks

Instance names unique names used by database notification services to locate instance resources

Packet sniffing the process of capturing packets traveling through a network and analyzing them

Port scanning the process of scanning a network or system to find accessible ports

SQL Server Resolution Service (SSRS) a service that provides referral services for multiple server instances running on the same machine

Introduction to Database Penetration Testing

Database penetration testing is the technique of testing a database for vulnerabilities to hacking attacks. This type of penetration testing uses techniques designed to address general database vulnerabilities as well as specific database issues such as those related to Microsoft SQL or Oracle servers. Techniques such as port scanning are important for database penetration testing. This chapter teaches you about the techniques involved in database penetration testing.

Port Scanning

Port scanning is the process of scanning a network or system to find accessible ports. It is a basic technique used in database penetration, so familiarity with port-scanning techniques is important.

Basic Techniques

The basic port scan tries to find which port is open or available to probe. The following techniques are basic port scans:

- *TCP connect()*: The TCP connect() system call provided by an OS is used to open a connection to any port on a machine. If the port is listening, connect() will succeed.
- *Strobe*: Strobe is a narrower scanning technique. It scans for only intended ports, unlike other port-scanning techniques that scan all available ports. Attackers use strobe to scan only those services that are exploitable.

Advanced Techniques

The following are some advanced port-scanning techniques:

- *Fragmented packet port scan*: This scan divides a TCP header into many IP fragments, enabling TCP packets to bypass firewall filters because a complete TCP header that can match their filter rules is not available. Some packet filters and firewalls can queue IP fragments until the entire header is available, but this degrades network performance, so most do not.
- *SYN scan*: This is also referred to as half-open scanning, because a TCP connection is not opened completely. To open a connection, a SYN packet is sent and a response is awaited. If a response SYN/ACK is received, then it indicates that the port is listening. If an RST packet is received, that indicates the port is not listening.
- *FIN scan*: This type of scanning sends FIN packets to ports. A closed port responds to a FIN message with an RST packet. Open ports, however, will typically silently drop the FIN packet. Thus, an attacker can identify an open port by sending a FIN packet and noting if a response is not received.
- *Bounce scan*: FTP protocol vulnerabilities can be found with FTP bounce scanning. This type of scan requires support for proxy FTP connections and is similar to IP spoofing.
- *Finger*: This technique takes advantage of a finger server's support for recursive queries and its ability to allow commands to be sent through it. The query abc@xyz@123 will ask 123 to resolve abc@xyz. Attackers can use this technique to hide the original source of the request.
- *UDP scanning*: To find a UDP port, attackers start sending empty UDP datagrams. If the port is open, then the port sends an error message or just ignores the incoming datagrams. If the ports are closed, then the operating system sends an "ICMP Port Unreachable" message.
- *ICMP scan*: This is not exactly a port-scanning technique, because ICMP does not use ports. However, it can be useful to try pinging all hosts on a network to see if they respond. This is a quick way to develop an initial list of active hosts.
- *Fingerprinting an OS*: This technique is used to determine what operating system is running on a target host. The attacker sends unusual data to the host, and then he or she interprets the responses. Systems tend to respond differently to bad data, so the attacker can determine which operating system is running on the host, based on the responses.

Database Penetration Testing Steps

1. Scan for default ports used by the database.
2. Scan for nondefault ports used by the database.
3. Identify the instance names used by the database.

4. Identify the version number of the database.

5. Attempt to brute-force password hashes from the database.

6. Sniff database-related traffic on the local wire.

7. Test Microsoft SQL Server:

  - Test for direct access interrogation.
  - Scan for Microsoft SQL Server ports (TCP/UDP 1433).
  - Test for SQL Server Resolution Service (SSRS).
  - Test for buffer overflow in pwdencrypt() function.
  - Test for heap/stack buffer overflows in SSRS.
  - Test for buffer overflows in extended stored procedures.
  - Test for service account registry key.
  - Test for SQL injection attack vulnerability.
  - Test for blind SQL injection attack vulnerability.
  - Test for vulnerability to Google hacks.
  - Attempt direct-exploit attacks.
  - Try to retrieve server account list.
  - Use osql to test for default/common passwords.
  - Try to retrieve the sysxlogins table.
  - Brute-force the SA account.

8. Test Oracle Server:

  - Port-scan UDP/TCP ports (TCP/UDP 1433).
  - Check the status of TNS Listener running on the Oracle Server.
  - Try to log in using default account passwords.
  - Try to enumerate SIDs.
  - Use SQL*Plus to enumerate system tables.

9. Test MySQL Server:

  - Port-scan UDP/TCP ports.
  - Extract the version of the database being used.
  - Try to log in using default/common passwords.
  - Use a dictionary attack to try to break into accounts.
  - Extract system and user tables from the database.

Step 1: Scan for Default Ports Used by the Database

In this step, testers use port-scanning tools such as Nmap to scan for ports used by the database. The default ports in Figure 4-1 are used for various products such as Oracle Database and Oracle Application Server.

Step 2: Scan for Nondefault Ports Used by the Database

Figure 4-2 shows the nondefault ports used by Oracle.

Step 3: Identify the Instance Names Used by the Database

Instance names are unique names used by database notification services to locate instance resources. In Microsoft SQL Server, Notification Services uses the instance name to construct the instance database name

Service	Port	Product	How to change
Oracle HTTP Server listen port / Oracle HTTP Server port	80	Oracle Application Server	Edit httpd.conf and restart OHS
Oracle Internet Directory(non-SSL)	389	Oracle Application Server	
Oracle HTTP Server SSL port	443	Oracle Application Server	Edit httpd.conf and restart OHS
Oracle Internet Directory(SSL)	636	Oracle Application Server	
Oracle Net Listener / Enterprise Manager Repository port	1521	Oracle Application Server / Oracle Database	Edit listener.ora and restart listener
Oracle Net Listener	1526	Oracle Database	Edit listener.ora and restart listener
Oracle Names	1575	Oracle Database	Edit names.ora and restart names server
Oracle Connection Manager (CMAN)	1630	Oracle Connection Manager	Edit cman.ora and restart Connection Manager
Oracle JDBC for Rdb Thin Server	1701	Oracle Rdb	
Oracle Intelligent Agent	1748	Oracle Application Server	snmp_rw.ora
Oracle Intelligent Agent	1754	Oracle Application Server	snmp_rw.ora
Oracle Intelligent Agent	1808	Oracle Application Server	snmp_rw.ora
Oracle OC4J IIOPS1	3501	Oracle Application Server	
Oracle OC4J IIOPS2	3601	Oracle Application Server	
Oracle OC4J JMS	3701	Oracle Application Server	
Oracle9iAS Web Cache Admin port	4000	Oracle Application Server	Webcache Admin GUI or webcache.xml
Oracle9iAS Web Cache Invalidation port	4001	Oracle Application Server	Webcache Admin GUI or webcache.xml
Oracle9iAS Web Cache Statistics port	4002	Oracle Application Server	Webcache Admin GUI or webcache.xml
Oracle Internet Directory(SSL)	4031	Oracle Application Server	
Oracle Internet Directory(non-SSL)	4032	Oracle Application Server	
OracleAS Certificate Authority (OCA) - Server Authentication	4400	Oracle Application Server	
OracleAS Certificate Authority (OCA) - Mutual Authentication	4401	Oracle Application Server	
Oracle HTTP Server SSL port	4443	Oracle Application Server	Edit httpd.conf and restart OHS
Oracle9iAS Web Cache HTTP Listen(SSL) port	4444	Oracle Application Server	Webcache Admin GUI or webcache.xml
Oracle TimesTen	4662	Oracle TimesTen	
Oracle TimesTen	4758	Oracle TimesTen	
Oracle TimesTen	4759	Oracle TimesTen	
Oracle TimesTen	4761	Oracle TimesTen	
Enterprise Manager Reporting port	3339	Oracle Application Server	Edit oem_webstage/oem.conf and restart OHS
Oracle OC4J IIOP	3401	Oracle Application Server	

Figure 4-1 These ports are the default ports used in products such as Oracle Database and Oracle Application Server.

Oracle TimesTen	4764	Oracle TimesTen	
Oracle TimesTen	4766	Oracle TimesTen	
Oracle TimesTen	4767	Oracle TimesTen	
Oracle Enterprise Manager Web Console	5500	Oracle Enterprise Manager Web	
iSQLPlus 10g	5560	Oracle i*SQLPlus	
iSQLPlus 10g	5580	Oracle i*SQLPlus RMI Port	
Oracle Notification Service request port	6003	Oracle Application Server	
Oracle Notification Service local port	6100	Oracle Application Server	
Oracle Notification Service remote port	6200	Oracle Application Server	
Oracle9iAS Clickstream Collector Agent	6668	Oracle Application Server	
Java Object Cache port	7000	Oracle Application Server	
DCM Java Object Cache port	7100	Oracle Application Server	
Oracle HTTP Server Diagnostic Port	7200	Oracle Application Server	
Oracle HTTP Server Port Tunneling	7501	Oracle Application Server	
Oracle HTTP Server listen port / Oracle HTTP Server port	7777	Oracle Application Server	Edit httpd.conf and restart OHS
Oracle9iAS Web Cache HTTP Listen(non-SSL) port	7779	Oracle Application Server	Webcache Admin GUI or webcache.xml
Oracle HTTP Server Jserv port	8007	Oracle Application Server	
Oracle XMLDB HTTP port	8080	Oracle Database	change dbms_xdb.cfg_update
OC4J Forms / Reports Instance	8888	Oracle Developer Suite	
OC4J Forms / Reports Instance	8889	Oracle Developer Suite	
Oracle Forms Server 6 / 6i	9000	Oracle Application Server	
Oracle SOAP Server	9998	Oracle Application Server	
OS Agent	14000	Oracle Application Server	
Oracle TimesTen	15000	Oracle TimesTen	
Oracle TimesTen	15002	Oracle TimesTen	
Oracle TimesTen	15004	Oracle TimesTen	
Log Loader	44000	Oracle Enterprise Manager	

Figure 4-1   These ports are the default ports used in products such as Oracle Database and Oracle Application Server.   (*continued*)

if the database instance name is not specified. In this case, the name of the instance database is of the form <instanceName>NSMain. The following points should be addressed while specifying an instance name:

- Specify a unique name so that instance resources can be identified easily.
- Instance names must be kept short and be based on unchanging entities.
- Databases support multiple instances, but only one instance can be a default instance.
- Instance names are not case-sensitive.

Service	Port	Notes
sql*net	66	Oracle SQL*NET
SQL*Net 1	1525	Registered as orasrv
tlisrv	1527	-
coauthor	1529	-
Oracle Remote Data Base	1571	rdb-dbs-disp
oracle-em1	1748	-
oracle-em2	1754	-
Oracle-VP2	1808	-
Oracle-VP1	1809	-

Service	Port	Notes
oracle?	2005	Registered as "berknet" for 2005 TCP, oracle for 2005 UDP
Oracle GIOP	2481	giop
Oracle GIOP SSL	2482	giop-ssl
Oracle TTC	2483	ttc. Oracle may use this port to replace 1521 in future
Oracle TTC SSL	2484	ttc-ssl
OEM Agent	3872	Oem-agent
Oracle RTC-PM port	3891	rtc-pm-port
Oracle dbControl Agent	3938	dbcontrol_agent

Figure 4-2   This chart shows nondefault ports used by Oracle.

Step 4: Identify the Version Number of the Database

The following methods can be used to get the version number of installed Oracle products:

- Connect and log in to the Oracle database with SQL*Plus. Upon login, text like the following will appear: "SQL*Plus: Release 9.2.0.6.0 - Production on Tue Oct 18 17:58:57 2005 Copyright (c) 1982, 2002, Oracle Corporation. All rights reserved. Connected to: Oracle9i Enterprise Edition Release 9.2.0.6.0 - 64bit Production With the Partitioning, OLAP and Oracle Data Mining options JServer Release 9.2.0.6.0 - Production." The number after "Oracle9i Enterprise Edition Release" is the version of the Oracle database.

- Retrieve the version information from the v$version table by using SQL*Plus. This table shows version information on Oracle, PL/SQL, etc. To retrieve the version information for Oracle, testers can execute the following SQL statement:

```
select * from v$version where banner like 'Oracle%
```

It should return something like the following output:

```
Banner

_____

Oracle9i Enterprise Edition Release 9.2.0.1.0 - 64bit Production
```

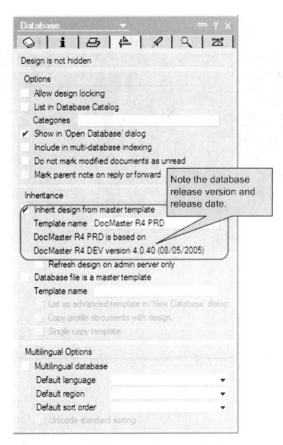

Figure 4-3 Information about a database can be found in the Oracle Universal Installer.

- Version information can also be checked from Installed Products from the Oracle Universal Installer. This tells what products are installed on the machine and also the products' version information. In UNIX, the installer is located at $ORACLE_HOME/bin/runInstaller. In Windows, the installer can be accessed by clicking **Start,** then **All Programs,** then **Oracle Installed Products,** and finally **Universal Installer,** as shown in Figure 4-3.

Step 5: Attempt to Brute-Force Password Hashes from the Database

Brute-forcing is the process of trying every possible password combination until one of them works. Penetration testers can use tools such as Orabf to brute-force password hashes. Orabf, shown in Figure 4-4, is a brute-force/ dictionary tool for Oracle hashes. The speed of Orabf is dependent on the length of the username and the length of the password it's trying.

Step 6: Sniff Database-Related Traffic on the Local Wire

Packet sniffing is the process of capturing packets traveling through a network and analyzing them. Sniffing can determine the number of database connections. Network and database administrators can legitimately use sniffing to check the availability of network devices and databases, and to control the quality of traffic flowing through the network. However, attackers can also use sniffing techniques to steal sensitive information from the network. There are various packet-sniffing tools available, such as Ethereal, that can be used to sniff data packets from a network.

Step 7: Test Microsoft SQL Server

Step 7.1: Test for Direct Access Interrogation

Direct or ad hoc access enables users to directly access the underlying data structures. Direct database access is generally controlled by the security policy of an organization. Testers need to try to bypass the authentication

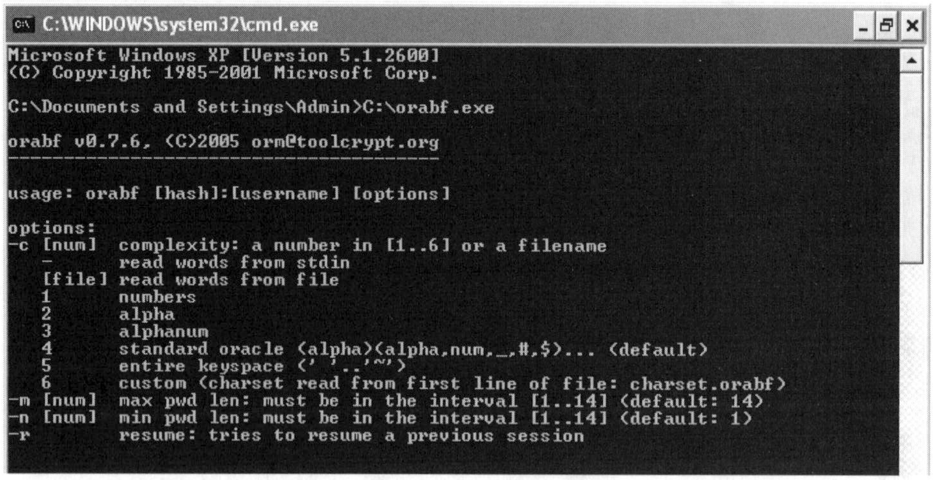

Figure 4-4   Orabf is a brute-force tool for Oracle hashes.

mechanism that has been implemented to protect the database from fraudulent use. Testers can try to query common database fields to see if they can access the data directly.

Step 7.2: Scan for Microsoft SQL Server Ports (TCP/UDP 1433)

Microsoft SQL Server, including the desktop editions that are often silently installed with other Microsoft applications, opens and services queries delivered over incoming TCP connections through port 1433. Testers can use a port-scanning tool to scan port 1433 for Microsoft SQL Server services.

Step 7.3: Test for SQL Server Resolution Service (SSRS)

SQL Server Resolution Service (SSRS) is used to provide referral services for multiple server instances running on the same machine. It listens to requests on UDP port 1434, returning the address and port number of an SQL Server instance and providing access to the database requested. SSRS not only provides referrals but also replies to the ping messages of other SQL Servers and marks their presence on the network. SSRS can be discovered through the following methods:

- Scanning UDP port 1434 for SQL Server Resolution Service (SSRS)
- Pinging UDP port 1434 from another SQL Server; a reply confirms SSRS

Step 7.4: Test for Buffer Overflow in pwdencrypt() Function

User information such as usernames and passwords are stored in the SQL Server. At the time of login, the pwdencrypt() function compares the user-supplied password with the stored password. A buffer overflow in the pwdencrypt() function permits hackers or unauthorized users to run arbitrary code with the rights of the SQL service account. Penetration testers should send a very long password to check to make sure the SQL Server's pwdencrypt() function is not vulnerable to buffer overflows.

Step 7.5: Test for Heap/Stack Buffer Overflows in SSRS

SSRS provides many services for various server instances operating on a single machine. SSRS can be vulnerable to a heap/stack buffer overflow that allows unauthorized users to run random code by sending a crafted request to UDP port 1434. The random code runs by sending an illegal request to the port. The server host executes the requested code with the rights of the SQL Server's service account. Penetration testers should try to send such a request to port 1434 and see if a buffer overflow occurs.

Step 7.6: Test for Buffer Overflows in Extended Stored Procedures

Microsoft SQL Server contains many extended stored procedures to execute a set of server commands together. Many extended stored procedures cause stack buffer overflows and permit public access. Testers should try to load and run a database query that may call one of the affected procedures.

Step 7.7: Test for Service Account Registry Key

Microsoft SQL Server runs under the service account that is defined by the administrator at the time of installation. All the defined service accounts are stored in the registry of the SQL Server. Only the system administrator has the permission to alter or change the defined value of the registry key. But access to the xp_regwrite() procedure, which is one of the extended stored procedures, can change the registry key. This allows the SQL Server to use another account as its service account, and an attacker can run any query or command with the rights of the operating system.

Step 7.8: Test for SQL Injection Attack Vulnerability

SQL injection attacks are executed using front-end Web applications. In this attack, SQL queries and SQL commands are directly inserted into a Web site's URL. An SQL injection attack enables the attacker to read the details of the database. Testers can write special queries like the following to attempt to gain access to the database:

```
EXISTS(SELECT * FROM users WHERE name='jake' AND password LIKE
'%w%') AND ''='
EXISTS(SELECT * FROM users WHERE name='jake' AND password LIKE
'_ _w%') AND ''='
```

Automated tools such as SQL Injector, seen in Figure 4-5, can be used to execute injection attacks.

Figure 4-5   Tools such as SQL Injector can be used to execute injection attacks.

Step 7.9: Test for Blind SQL Injection Attack Vulnerability

A blind SQL injection attack enables an unauthorized user to exploit Web applications and back-end SQL Servers. In this attack, the user does not receive any feedback or error messages from the Web server. Testers can use the program Absinthe (Figure 4-6) to attempt to exploit a Web application.

Step 7.10: Test for Vulnerability to Google Hacks

Google hacks use the Google search engine to find vulnerabilities, publicly accessible events, and primary operating systems of SQL Servers. Testers can use Google queries such as those available in the Google Hacking Database.

Step 7.11: Attempt Direct-Exploit Attacks

Direct-exploit attacks allow the user to perform code injection and gain unauthorized command-line access. Penetration testers can use Metasploit (Figure 4-7) to conduct a direct-exploit attack. This tool has exploit code for many vulnerabilities, Web servers, and operating systems.

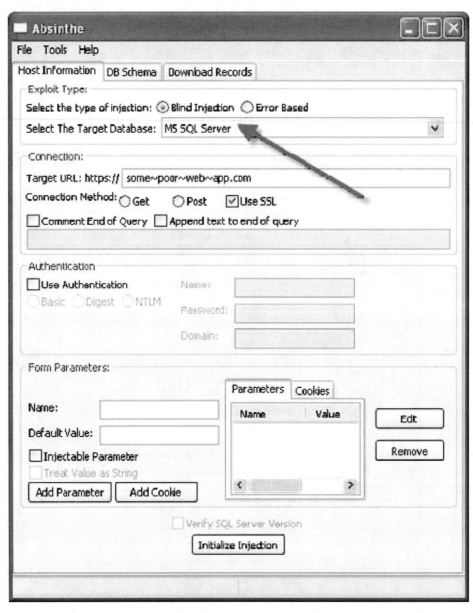

Figure 4-6   Use the program Absinthe to attempt to exploit a Web application.

Step 7.12: Try to Retrieve Server Account List

A server account list includes the SQL login IDs and data about the server. Normal users are not allowed to see this information. Testers can try to use the code in Figure 4-8 to access the account list.
Figure 4-9 shows the output of running this code.

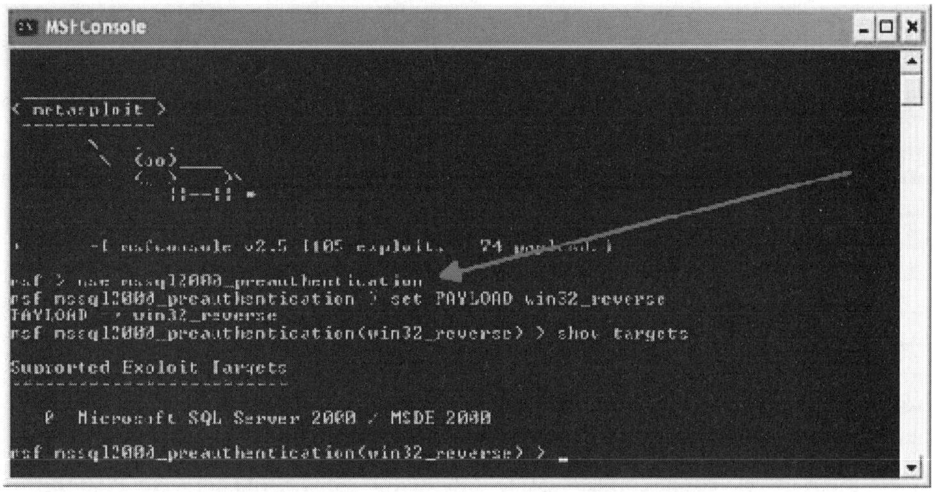

Figure 4-7   Metasploit can be used to conduct a direct-exploit attack.

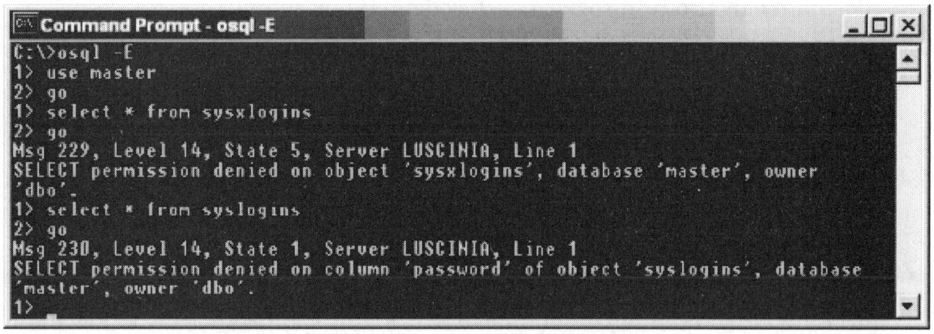

Figure 4-8   A server account list can be retrieved with the use of specific code.

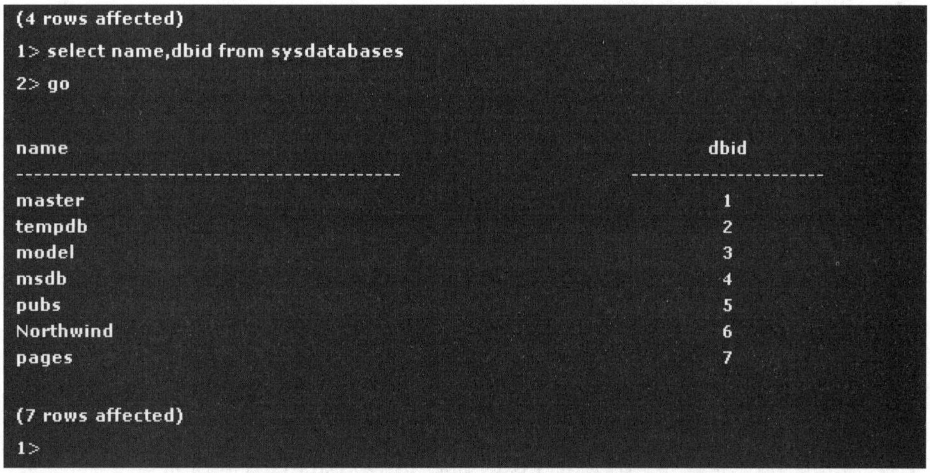

Figure 4-9   A server account list can reveal SQL login IDs and data about the server.

System table	Database	Function
sysxlogins	master	Contains one row for each login account that can connect to SQL Server. If you need to access information in sysxlogins, you should do so through the syslogins view.
sysmessages	master	Contains one row for each system error or warning that SQL Server can return.
sysdatabases	master	Contains one row for each database on a SQL Server.
sysusers	All	Contains one row for each Windows NT user, Windows NT group, SQL Server user, or SQL Server role in a database.
sysobjects	All	Contains one row for each object in a data base, such as tables, constraints, rules, and stored procedures.

Figure 4-10   The sysxlogins system table maintains a list of fully qualified names of users and groups.

Step 7.13: Use osql to Test for Default/Common Passwords

The osql utility is a Microsoft command prompt utility used for ad hoc, interactive execution of Transact-SQL statements and scripts. The osql utility is typically used in the following ways:

- Users interactively enter Transact-SQL statements. The results are displayed in the command prompt window.
- Users submit an osql job, either specifying a single Transact-SQL statement to execute or pointing the utility to a text file that contains Transact-SQL statements to execute. The output is usually directed to a text file, but it can also be displayed in the command prompt window.

Step 7.14: Try to Retrieve the Sysxlogins Table

The sysxlogins table (Figure 4-10) in SQL Server 2000 maintains a list of fully qualified names of users and groups for performance reasons. The table is queried first to retrieve the login name and SID of the user, using the SUSER_SNAME() and SUSER_SID() functions. If the sysxlogins table does not match the requested username or SID, then the Windows Local Security Authority (LSA) is queried for the information.

Step 7.15: Brute-Force the SA Account

SA is a built-in SQL Server database administrator login. Databases can be logged into using the SA login by cracking passwords using techniques such as brute-forcing. Password-cracking tools, such as THC Hydra (Figure 4-11), can be used to brute-force an SA login password.

Step 8: Test Oracle Server

Step 8.1: Port-Scan UDP/TCP Ports (TCP/UDP 1433)

Testers can use a port-scanning tool, such as NmapNT, to scan for port 1433, as shown in Figure 4-12.

Step 8.2: Check the Status of TNS Listener Running on the Oracle Server

The TNS Listener process is an independent process that connects databases and resides in the software layer of both the client and server. TNS Listener establishes connections between the Oracle Server and a client application, allowing valid users who have permissions to control the database and OS to execute arbitrary code, as shown in Figure 4-13.

TNS Listener can be configured in one of three modes:

1. *Database*: Provides network access to an Oracle database instance
2. *PLSExtProc*: Method for PL/SQL packages to access operating system executables
3. *Executable*: Provides network access to operating system executables

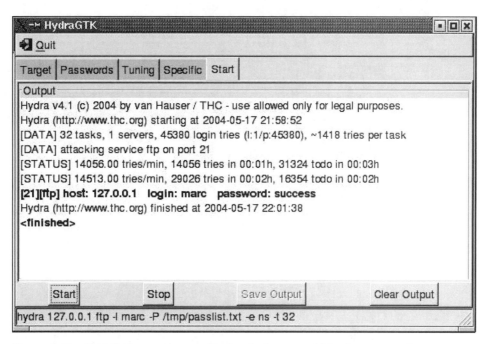

Figure 4-11   THC Hydra can be used to brute-force an SA login password.

Figure 4-12   Nmap can be used to scan for port 1433.

- To find the TNS Listener, testers can use port scanners such as Nmap and Amap.
- If the TNS Listener is not password protected, the following command can be used to get the SID:

      tnscmd10g.pl status -h <ip-address>

- The following files control the Listener:
  - *$ORACLE_HOME/bin/lsnrctl*: This is the actual TNS Listener control program.
  - *$ORACLE_HOME/network/admin/listener.ora*: This is the actual TNS Listener configuration file.
  - *$ORACLE_HOME/bin/tnslnsr*: This is the actual listening process.

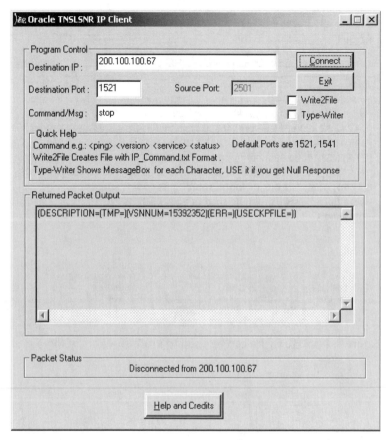

Figure 4-13 TNS Listener establishes connections between the Oracle Server and a client application.

Step 8.3: Try to Log in Using Default Account Passwords

Figure 4-14 shows a list of default account passwords that testers can use to attempt to access a database if the default password was not changed.

Step 8.4: Try to Enumerate SIDs

Testers can use the OraclePwGuess utility (Figure 4-15) of Oracle Auditing Tools (OAT) to enumerate default usernames and passwords.

Step 8.5: Use SQL*Plus to Enumerate System Tables

SQL*Plus runs .sql scripts against Oracle. Penetration testers can run WinSID or a similar tool to look for the service name. To establish a connection to a remote server, testers can go to the command prompt and type the following (Figure 4-16):

```
sqlplus <user>/<password>@<test.domain>
```

Then from the SQL> prompt, testers type the following:

```
@c:\sql\sql
```

(In this example, the script is located at c:\sql and is called sql.sql.)

Step 9: Test MySQL Server

Step 9.1: Port-Scan UDP/TCP Ports

Testers can use port-scanning tools, such as Nmap, to scan TCP/UDP ports for MySQL Server database services.

#INTERNAL	ORACLE
#INTERNAL	SYS_STNT
ABM	ABM
ADAMS	WOOD
ADLDEMO	ADLDEMO
ADMIN	JETSPEED
ADMIN	WELCOME
ADMINISTRATOR	ADMIN
ADMINISTRATOR	ADMINISTRATOR
AHL	AHL
AHM	AHM
AK	AK
ALHRO	XXX
ALHRW	XXX
ALR	ALR
AMS	AMS
AMV	AMV
ANDY	SWORDFISH
ANONYMOUS	ANONYMOUS
ANONYMOUS	<INVALID>
AP	AP
APPLMGR	APPLMGR
APPLSYS	APPLSYS
APPLSYS	APPS
APPLSYS	FND
APPLSYSPUB	APPLSYSPUB
APPLSYSPUB	PUB
APPLSYSPUB	FNDPUB
APPLYSYSPUB	FNDPUB
APPLYSYSPUB	PUB
APPLYSYSPUB	<UNKNOWN>
APPS	APPS
APPS_MRC	APPS
APPUSER	APPPASSWORD
AQ	AQ
AQDEMO	AQDEMO
AQJAVA	AQJAVA
AQUSER	AQUSER
AR	AR
ASF	ASF
ASG	ASG
ASL	ASL
ASO	ASO
ASP	ASP
AST	AST
ATM	SAMPLEATM
AUDIOUSER	AUDIOUSER
AURORAJISUTILITY$	<INVALID>
AURORAJISUTILITY$	INVALID
AURORAORBUNAUTHENTICATED	INVALID
AURORAORBUNAUTHENTICATED	<INVALID>
AX	AX
AZ	AZ
BC4J	BC4J
BEN	BEN
BIC	BIC
BIL	BIL
BIM	BIM
BIS	BIS
BIV	BIV
BIX	BIX
BLAKE	PAPER
BLEWIS	BLEWIS
BOM	BOM
BRIO_ADMIN	BRIO_ADMIN
BRUGERNAVN	ADGANGSKODE
BRUKERNAVN	PASSWORD
BSC	BSC
BUG_REPORTS	BUG_REPORTS
CALVIN	HOBBES
CATALOG	CATALOG
CCT	CCT
CDEMO82	CDEMO82
CDEMO82	CDEMO83
CDEMO82	UNKNOWN
CDEMOCOR	CDEMOCOR
CDEMORID	CDEMORID
CDEMOUCB	CDEMOUCB
CDOUGLAS	CDOUGLAS
CE	CE
CENTRA	CENTRA

Figure 4-14 If the default password was not changed, then it can be used to access a database.

```
C:\Oracle\oat>opwg
        Oracle Password Guesser v1.3.1 by patrik@cqure.net
        ----------------------------------------------------
        OraclePwGuess [options]
                -s*     <servername>
                -u      <userfile>
                -p      <passfile>
                -d      <SID>
                -P      <portnr>
                -D      disables default pw checks
                -C      check for CREATE LIBRARY permissions
                -v      be verbose
[root@localhost oat]# sh opwg.sh -s 200.100.100.218 OR c:\opwg -s
200.100.100.218
Oracle Password Guesser v1.3.1 by patrik@cqure.net
-------------------------------------------------
Skipping PLSExtProc ...
INFO: Running pwcheck on SID test
Successfully logged in with DBSNMP/DBSNMP
Successfully logged in with SCOTT/TIGER
```

Figure 4-15   OraclePwGuess can enumerate default usernames and passwords.

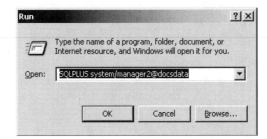

Figure 4-16   This command will establish a connection to the remote.

Step 9.2: Extract the Version of the Database Being Used

SQLver can extract the version by querying the file snetlib.dll without logging into servers. The following is the syntax for this command:

```
sqlver <ip _ address/hostname> <port _ number>
```

Step 9.3: Try to Login Using Default/Common Passwords

Figure 4-17 depicts some common/default passwords that a tester can use to log in.

Step 9.4: Use a Dictionary Attack to Try to Break Into Accounts

A method to break password-based security systems is by running a dictionary attack. The following tools can be used to conduct dictionary attacks:

- Cain & Abel
- SQLdict
- John the Ripper
- THC Hydra
- Aircrack
- L0phtCrack

Manufacturer	Product	Version	Protocol	User ID	Password	Access
Zcom	Wireless		SNMP	root	admin	Admin
Zoom	ADSL Modem		Console	admin	zoomadsl	Admin
Zeus	Admin Server	4.1r2	HTTP	admin		
Zyxel	ADSL routers	ZyNOS	Multi	admin	1234	Admin
Zyxel	Prestige		HTTP	n/a	1234	Admin
Zyxel	Prestige		FTP	root	1234	Admin
Zyxel	Prestige		Telnet	(none)	1234	Admin
Zyxel	Prestige 100IH		Console	n/a	1234	Admin
Zyxel	Prestige 324		Multi	n/a	(none)	Admin
Zyxel	Prestige 643		Console	(none)	1234	Admin
Zyxel	Prestige 650		Multi	1234	1234	Admin
Zyxel	Prestige 652HW-31 ADSL Router		HTTP	admin	1234	Admin
Zyxel	ZyWall 2		HTTP	n/a	(none)	Admin

Figure 4-17   Common default passwords can sometimes be used to log in to a database.

- AirSnort
- SolarWinds
- Pwdump
- RainbowCrack
- Brutus

Cain & Abel   Cain & Abel (Figure 4-18) is a password recovery tool. Its main purpose is simplified recovery of passwords and credentials from various sources. Cain & Abel recovers passwords through the following techniques:

- Cracking encrypted passwords using a dictionary attack
- Brute-forcing and cryptanalysis attacks
- Recording VoIP conversations
- Decoding scrambled passwords
- Recovering wireless network keys
- Revealing password boxes
- Uncovering cached passwords
- Analyzing routing protocols

SQLdict   SQLdict (Figure 4-19) is a dictionary attack tool designed for SQL Server. This tool is used by specifying the IP address of the target, the username, and the appropriate wordlist to try (via the **Load Password File** button).

Step 9.5: Extract System and User Tables from the Database

User tables contain information such as hostnames, usernames, passwords, and privileges of particular users. To extract system and user tables, testers can go to User Administration from the database administration panel (Figure 4-20).

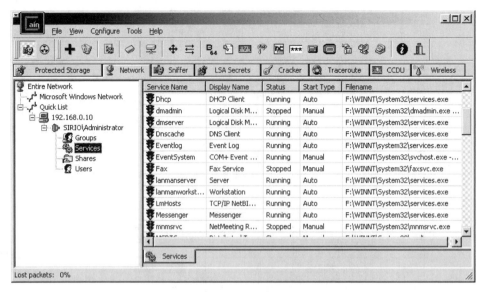

Figure 4-18 Cain & Abel is a password recovery tool.

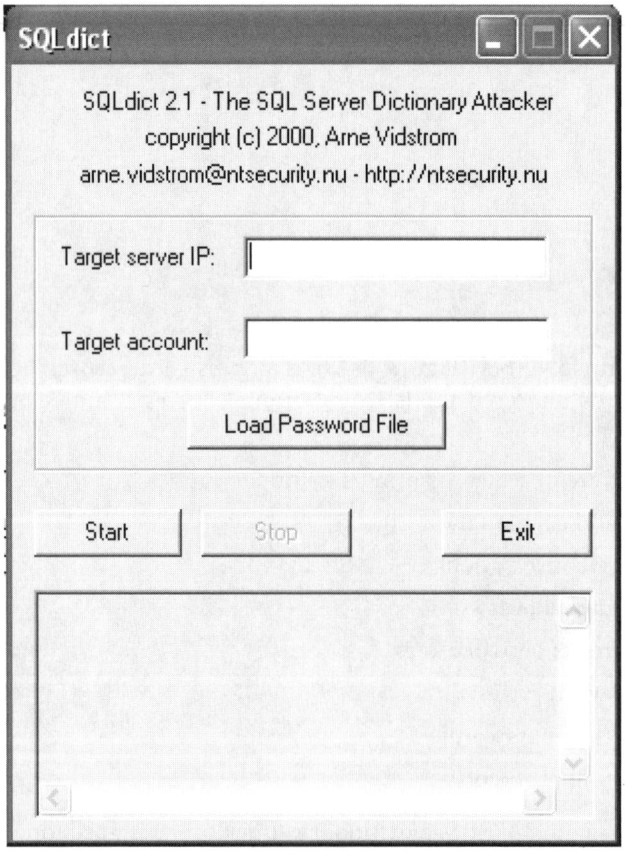

Figure 4-19 SQLdict is a dictionary attack tool
specifically designed for SQL Server.

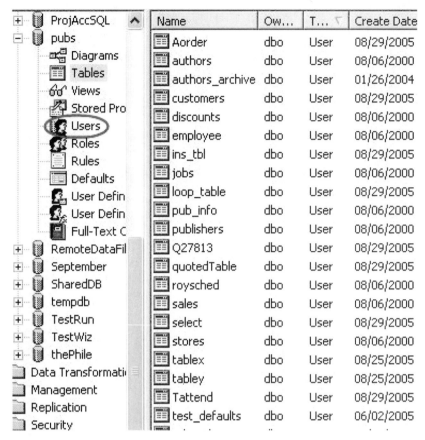

Figure 4-20 User tables contain information such as hostnames, usernames, passwords, and privileges of particular users.

Chapter Summary

- Port scanning is a basic technique used in database penetration, making familiarity with port-scanning techniques important.

- In Microsoft SQL Server, Notification Services uses the instance name to construct the instance database name, if the database instance name is not specified.

- Network and database administrators can legitimately use sniffing to check the availability of network devices and databases. They can also use it to control the quality of traffic flowing through the network.

- Microsoft SQL Server, including the desktop editions that are often silently installed with other Microsoft applications, opens and services queries delivered over incoming TCP connections through port 1433.

- Microsoft SQL Server contains many extended stored procedures to execute a set of server commands together. Many extended stored procedures cause stack buffer overflows and permit public access.

- Google hacks use the Google search engine to find vulnerabilities, publicly accessible events, and primary operating systems of SQL Servers.

Chapter 5

Virus and Trojan Detection

Objectives

After completing this chapter, you should be able to:

- Use connection and port information to detect Trojans
- Use process information to detect Trojans
- Detect boot-sector viruses
- Enumerate the different tools used to detect viruses and Trojans

Key Terms

Boot-sector virus   a virus that infects the boot sector of a computer system and is typically spread through an infected floppy

Introduction to Virus and Trojan Detection

Viruses and Trojans are two of the most widespread types of malicious software. Attackers use them to do anything from causing mischief to completely shutting a system down. There are a large number of existing viruses and Trojans, and new ones are being developed every day. Because of this, administrators need to be aware of how to detect and remove these pieces of malware. This chapter describes the steps that administrators can take to detect viruses and Trojans. It also lists many of the tools they can use to detect and eliminate malware.

Steps for Detecting Viruses and Trojans

The following are the steps for detecting Trojans and viruses in a system:

- *Step 1*: Use **netstat -a** to detect Trojan connections.
- *Step 2*: Check Windows Task Manager.

- *Step 3*: Check if scanning programs are enabled.
- *Step 4*: Check if antivirus and anti-Trojan programs are working.
- *Step 5*: Detect any boot-sector viruses.

Step 1: Use netstat -a to Detect Trojan Connections

Netstat is used to display active TCP connections, IP routing tables, and ports on which the computer is listening. Generally, most Trojans use TCP or UDP sockets. Netstat shows details about the different TCP connections, and administrators can then detect any suspicious connections that may indicate a Trojan. Sometimes, firewalls, routers, and IDS affect the port-scanning results. The syntax for Netstat is **netstat [options] [-p protocol] [interval]**.

The options for Netstat include the following:

- *-a*: Display all connections and listening ports
- *-e*: Display Ethernet statistics
- *-n*: Display addresses and port numbers in numerical form
- *-r*: Display the routing table
- *-p*: Show only connections for the protocol specified; may be either TCP or UDP
- *-s*: Display per-protocol statistics; by default, statistics are shown for IP, ICMP, TCP, and UDP

Figure 5-1 shows the output of **netstat -a**.

Step 2: Check Windows Task Manager

Windows Task Manager (Figure 5-2) provides detailed information about the applications and other processes running on a system. It also provides information about networking, performance, and users on the system. Administrators should check the Windows Task Manager for different applications running on the system. If they find any suspicious application running, they should check it to make sure it is not a virus or Trojan application.

Step 3: Check If Scanning Programs Are Enabled

Scanning is used to detect Trojans and viruses present on a system. Scanning is performed with the help of scanning tools, antivirus software, and anti-Trojan software. It is necessary to check whether the scanning programs are enabled or not. If they are disabled, the system is vulnerable to attack. Administrators should enable these programs.

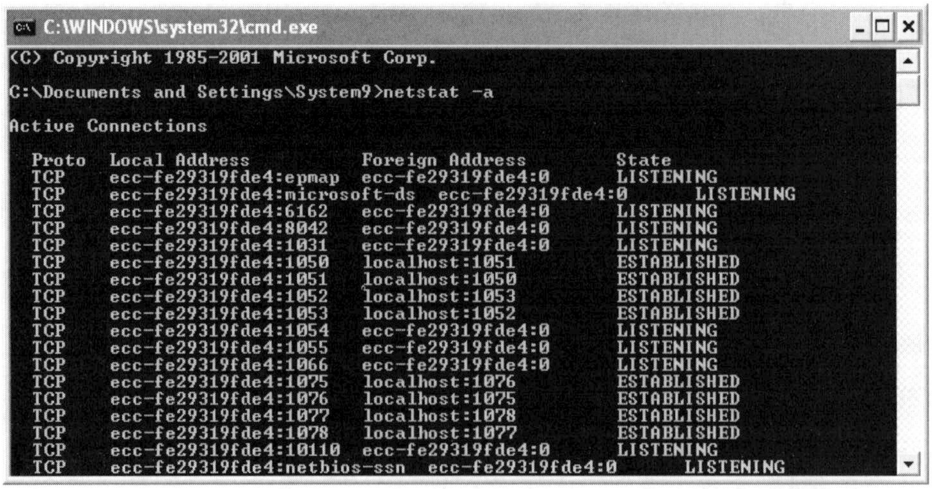

Figure 5-1   The **netstat -a** command shows all connections and listening ports.

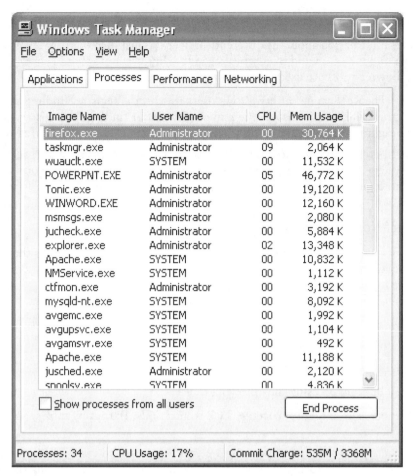

Figure 5-2 Windows Task Manager provides information about the applications and other processes running on a system.

The following are some of the scanning techniques:

- *Step 3.1*: Scan for suspicious running processes.
- *Step 3.2*: Scan for suspicious registry entries.
- *Step 3.3*: Check for suspicious open ports.
- *Step 3.4*: Scan for suspicious network activities.
- *Step 3.5*: Use HijackThis to scan for spyware.

Step 3.1: Scan for Suspicious Running Processes

A system should be scanned for any suspicious running process. This scanning can be done using the following scanning tools:

- *Process Viewer*: Process Viewer is a utility that displays detailed information about processes running under Windows. For each process, it displays memory, threads, and module usage. For each DLL, it shows full path and version information. It comes with a command-line version that allows the user to write scripts to check if a process is running, to kill it, and so on. The main window shows a list of running processes including information about the process ID, the priority, and the full path to the process module. The user can sort columns by clicking on the column header.

- *What's On My Computer?*: This tool helps a user easily access information about any file, folder, process, service, IP connection, module, or driver running on the computer. It protects against viruses, Trojans, spyware, and bad or poor-quality software. It provides additional information about the programs that are running on the user's computer.

Step 3.2: Scan for Suspicious Registry Entries

The registry stores information about the different applications installed on the system. To open Registry Editor, a user clicks **Start** and then **Run** and then types **regedit**. Administrators should check the registry for unknown .exe files. The following tools are used for scanning:

- *RegScanner*: The RegScanner utility allows users to scan the registry, find registry values that match the specified search criteria, and display them in one list. After finding the registry values, users can easily jump to the right value in Registry Editor simply by double-clicking the desired registry item.

- *MSConfig*: Microsoft System Configuration Utility is a tool that is used to troubleshoot problems with computer systems. It aids in editing and administering text-based configuration files such as win.ini and autoexec.bat. It ensures that computers will boot faster and crash less often. It automatically checks for Trojans.

Step 3.3: Check for Suspicious Open Ports

Suspicious open ports should be scanned. These are ports associated with services that a user is not running or persistent ephemeral ports. Ephemeral ports are normally short-term-use ports, and it would be suspicious for any of these ports to be left open for extended periods.

Note that port numbers are divided into three ranges:

1. *Well-known ports*: 0 through 1023
2. *Registered ports*: 1024 through 49151
3. *Ephemeral or private ports*: 49152 through 65535

These ports can be scanned using the following tools:

- *Netstat*: Netstat is used to display active TCP connections, IP routing tables, and ports on which the computer is listening.

- *FPort*: FPort supports Windows operating systems. It reports all open TCP/IP and UDP ports and maps them to the owning application. This is similar to the information seen using the **netstat -an** command. However, it also maps those ports to running processes with the PID, process name, and path.

- *TCPView*: TCPView (Figure 5-3) is a Windows program that shows detailed listings of all TCP and UDP endpoints on the system, including the local and remote addresses and the state of TCP connections. On Windows NT, 2000, and XP, TCPView also reports the name of the process that owns the endpoint.

Step 3.4: Scan for Suspicious Network Activities

The following tools can be used to scan for suspicious network activities on the system:

- *Ethereal*: Ethereal is a GUI network protocol analyzer. It allows the user to interactively browse packet data from a live network or from a previously saved capture file (Figure 5-4). Ethereal's native capture file format is libpcap format, which is also the format used by Tcpdump and various other tools. In addition, Ethereal can read capture files from Snoop and atmsnoop, Shomiti/Finisar Surveyor, Novell Analyzer, Network General/Network Associates DOS-based Sniffer (compressed or uncompressed), Microsoft Network Monitor, and so on.

- *Nessus*: Nessus is a network vulnerability scanner. It can perform a port scan, and it can run a comprehensive scan for network vulnerabilities.

- *Nmap*: Nmap is used for port scanning. It supports more than a dozen ways to scan a network. Some scanning techniques used are UDP, TCP connect, TCP SYN (half open), FTP proxy (bounce attack), reverse ident, ICMP (ping sweep), FIN, ACK sweep, Xmas Tree, SYN sweep, IP protocol, and null scan.

Step 3.5: Use HijackThis to Scan for Spyware

HijackThis (Figure 5-5) is a general browser hijacker detector and remover. This program detects general hijacking techniques that mainstream spyware removers do not detect. HijackThis examines certain key areas of the registry and hard drive, and lists their contents.

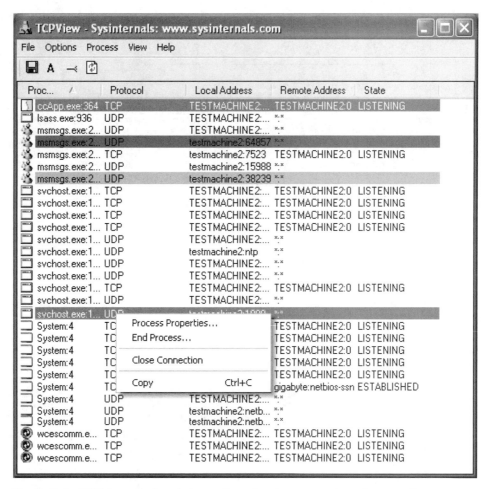

Figure 5-3 TCPView displays information about open ports and connections on a system.

Step 4: Check If Antivirus and Anti-Trojan Programs Are Working

Antivirus programs should be updated often to make sure they have the latest virus signatures. Most antivirus programs work by checking data and files against a database of known virus signatures. However, some programs merely look for viruslike processes, rather than specific viruses. Because of this, the user is just warned of a possible virus infection. This method can raise false alarms, so it is not considered as effective as the signature method.

Anti-Trojan software is specifically designed to detect Trojans. Most can be run alongside an antivirus program. However, no Trojan scanner is 100% effective, because manufacturers cannot keep up with the rapid evolution of Trojans. Therefore, the best practice is to update anti-Trojan software regularly.

Administrators should check to make sure these programs are updated and functioning properly. Some viruses are able to shut down antivirus software, and some can even make it look like the antivirus software is still running, making it important for administrators to remain vigilant.

Step 5: Detect Any Boot-Sector Viruses

Boot-sector viruses infect the boot sector of a computer system and are typically spread when users boot or attempt to boot from an infected floppy disk. Even if the disk does not contain the MS-DOS system files needed to successfully boot, an attempt to boot from an infected disk will load the virus into memory. The virus acts as if it were a device driver. The virus moves the Interrupt 12 return, allowing it to remain in memory even after a warm boot. The virus then infects the first hard disk in the system.

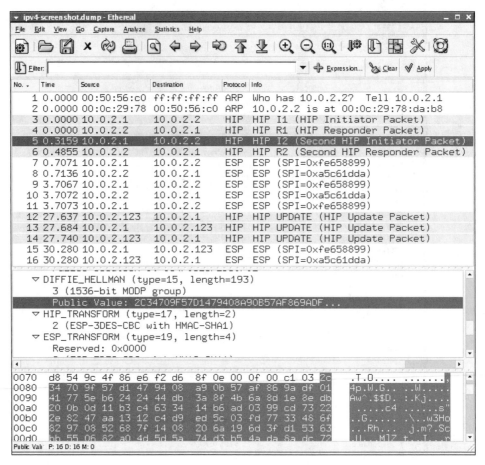

Figure 5-4 Ethereal allows a user to browse packet data drom a previously saved capture file.

Because the virus moves the Interrupt 12 return, the MS-DOS system memory will be 2 KB smaller than normal. This can be verified by running the MS-DOS chkdsk command.

Software

Spyware Detectors

Spyware detectors are used to detect spyware present on a system, and many can also attempt to remove the spyware. The following are some popular spyware detectors:

- Ad-Aware
- Spybot Search & Destroy
- PestPatrol
- McAfee Anti-Spyware
- SpywareGuard
- SpyCop
- Spyware Terminator
- XoftSpySE
- SPYWAREfighter

Figure 5-5 HijackThis scans key areas of the registry and presents a report based on that search.

Anti-Trojan Software

Anti-Trojan software is designed to detect Trojans. Most can be run alongside an antivirus program. The following are some popular anti-Trojan programs:

- Trojan Guard
- TrojanHunter
- ZoneAlarm
- WinPatrol
- LeakTest
- Kerio Personal Firewall
- Sub-Net
- TAVScan
- SpyBot Search & Destroy
- Anti Trojan
- Cleaner
- Comodo BOClean
- XoftSpySE
- Spyware Doctor

Antivirus Software

The following are some popular antivirus programs:

- Panda Antivirus
- AMacro AntiVirus
- BitDefender Professional Plus
- CyberScrub AntiVirus
- MDaemon
- AVG Antivirus
- Norton AntiVirus
- F-Secure Anti-Virus
- Kaspersky Anti-Virus
- AntiVir Personal
- Bootminder
- McAfee SecurityCenter
- CA Anti-Virus
- avast! Virus Cleaner

Chapter Summary

- The Netstat tool can detect open connections and listening ports that may indicate the presence of a Trojan on a system.
- Process Viewer, What's On My Computer? and HijackThis are some scanning tools.
- Boot-sector viruses are spread to computer systems when a user boots or attempts to boot from an infected floppy disk.
- Antivirus programs should be updated often to make sure they have the latest virus signatures.
- Spyware detectors are used to detect the spyware present on the system.

Chapter 6

Log Management Penetration Testing

Objectives

After completing this chapter, you should be able to:

- Understand log files
- Understand the need for log file management
- Understand the challenges in log file management
- Perform log file management penetration testing

Key Terms

Log a record of the events occurring within an organization's systems and networks

Log management the process of generating, transmitting, storing, analyzing, and disposing of log data

Syslog a client/server protocol that specifies a general log entry format and a log entry transport mechanism such as TCP or UDP

Introduction to Log Management Penetration Testing

A *log* is a record of the events occurring within an organization's systems and networks. Log files are important parts of an organization's computer systems. They provide administrators with important information that helps them optimize and troubleshoot all of the organization's computer components. It is important for the logging and log management mechanisms in the organization to function properly. It is also important to secure these log files, because attackers can use the information in them to attack the network. This chapter teaches you about log files, log file management, and how to perform a penetration test on an organization's log file management infrastructure.

Log File Overview

Log files maintain a record of all the events occurring in an organization's systems and networks. Log files were traditionally used solely for troubleshooting, but now they have become tools for organizations to perform the following tasks:

- Optimizing the performance of the system or the network
- Checking for malicious activities
- Maintaining records of all the actions for evidence purposes

Basically, logs are classified into the following two categories:

1. Security software logs
2. Operating system logs

Security software logs are logs that provide a record of security events. Security-related software typically triggers these security events. Some examples of security software are antimalware software, intrusion detection and prevention systems, remote access software, Web proxies, vulnerability management software, authentication servers, network quarantine servers, routers, and firewalls.

The following are some examples of security software log entries:

- *Intrusion detection system*: [**] [1:1407:9] SNMP trap udp [**] [Classification: Attempted Information Leak] [Priority: 2] 03/06-8:14:09.082119 192.168.1.167:1052 -> 172.30.128.27:162 UDP TTL:118 TOS:0x0 ID:29101 IpLen:20 DgmLen:87

- *Personal firewall*: 3/6/2006 8:14:07 AM,"Rule" "Block Windows File Sharing" "blocked (192.168.1.54, netbios-ssn(139)).", "Rule" "Block Windows File Sharing" "blocked (192.168.1.54, netbios-ssn(139)). Inbound TCP connection. Local address, service is (KENT(172.30.128.27), netbios-ssn(139)). Remote address, service is (192.168.1.54,39922). Process name is" "System"." 3/3/2006 9:04:04 AM, Firewall configuration updated: 398 rules., Firewall configuration updated: 398 rules.

- *Antispyware software*: DSO Exploit: Data source object exploit (Registry change, nothing done) HKEY_USERS\S-1-5-19\Software\Microsoft\Windows\CurrentVersion\Internet Settings\ Zones\0\1004!=W=3

Logs that record all events related to operating systems are operating system logs. Examples of these are system logs and audit records.

The Need for Log Management

Organizations use log data to strengthen information security with the help of advanced audits and data correlation. Log data are also used for troubleshooting and meeting compliance initiatives. *Log management* is the process of generating, transmitting, storing, analyzing, and disposing of log data. Effective log management provides the following security features:

- Ability to parse various log data formats
- Troubleshooting tools
- The capability to store and archive log data and perform robust searches against those logs
- Real-time and batch alerting processes to aid in incident response
- Detailed information about security records
- Auditing and forensic analysis to investigate malicious activity
- Routine log review and analysis that helps to identify and provide security against security threats, policy violations, operational problems, malicious activities, and so on

Challenges in Log Management

The following are some of the challenges faced in log management:

- Problems with the initial generation of log files due to incompatibility of various network devices
- Inconsistent log formats leading to a problem in storage of log files
- Maintenance of confidentiality, integrity, and availability of log data
- Inaccuracies in the system's internal clock, which prevent the proper logging of events
- Balancing the availability of a large amount of log information with the minimal availability of organizational resources for analysis
- Limited storage size for log data, which can lead to overwriting old data with new data or interrupted logging

Steps for Log Management Penetration Testing

The following are the steps for log management penetration testing:

- *Step 1*: Scan for log files.
- *Step 2*: Try to flood syslog servers with bogus log data.
- *Step 3*: Try malicious syslog message attacks (buffer overflows).
- *Step 4*: Perform a man-in-the-middle attack.
- *Step 5*: Check if the logs are encrypted.
- *Step 6*: Check if arbitrary data can be injected remotely into Microsoft ISA server log files.
- *Step 7*: Perform a DoS attack against Check Point FireWall-1's syslog daemon.
- *Step 8*: Send syslog messages containing escape sequences to Check Point FireWall-1's syslog daemon.

Step 1: Scan for Log Files

Testers can use different scanning tools to scan for log files. After finding the scanned files, testers can try to modify them to see if the system allows it. The following are log file scanning tools:

- Sawmill
- bcnumsg

Step 2: Try to Flood Syslog Servers with Bogus Log Data

Syslog is a client/server protocol that specifies a general log entry format and a log entry transport mechanism such as TCP or UDP. Most syslog applications use unreliable connectionless UDP protocols to move or rotate log information between hosts. UDP does not ensure or acknowledge that log entries are received successfully or in the correct sequence on the network.

Most syslog implementations do not perform any access control, so any host can send messages to a syslog server without caring about the capacity of the syslog server. A tester should try to send fake log data to a syslog server in large quantities and check for a denial of service that may occur due to flooding.

Step 3: Try Malicious Syslog Message Attacks (Buffer Overflows)

A buffer overflow is a condition that results from a programming error. If an application receives data and tries to store those data in a buffer that is too small to hold the data, the buffer can overflow. Bounds checking can prevent buffer overflows. If an attacker successfully overflows a buffer, he or she can cause a denial of service or can even cause the application to execute the attacker's own code. An attacker can send overly long messages to a syslog server to cause a buffer overflow.

Step 4: Perform a Man-In-The-Middle Attack

In a man-in–the-middle (MITM) attack, the attacker creates independent connections with the target systems and relays messages between them, making the targets believe that they are communicating directly with each other when, in fact, the attacker is controlling the whole conversation. This type of attack may be used to modify or destroy syslog messages in transit.

To perform a penetration test using a man-in-the-middle attack, testers should check the following:

- Whether the syslog client checks for the server's identity as presented in the server's certificate message before sending log files
- The client's local .ssh/known_hosts file if an SSH tunnel is used for log transmissions

Step 5: Check If the Logs Are Encrypted

Encryption is used for securing information. Log files can be protected with the help of encryption. Testers should check whether log files are encrypted or not. During transactions, syslog cannot encrypt log information.

Step 6: Check If Arbitrary Data Can Be Injected Remotely into Microsoft ISA Server Log Files

To inject arbitrary data remotely into a Microsoft ISA (Internet Security and Acceleration) server log file, a tester can send the following specially crafted HTTP request to modify the destination's host parameter in the log file:

```
GET / HTTP/1.0
Host: %01%02%03%04
Transfer-Encoding: whatever
```

In this case, the four ASCII characters 1, 2, 3, and 4 are injected into the destination's host parameter in the log file.

Step 7: Perform a DoS Attack Against Check Point FireWall-1's Syslog Daemon

The following are the steps for performing a DoS attack against Check Point FireWall-1 syslog daemon:

1. Start syslogd by enabling the firewall object.
2. Check for listening syslogd.
3. Send a valid syslog message from the remote host.
4. Send a random payload through syslog using the following command: **cat /dev/urandom | nc -u firewall 514**

Step 8: Send Syslog Messages Containing Escape Sequences to Check Point FireWall-1's Syslog Daemon

For this test, send syslog messages containing escape sequences to Check Point Firewall-1's syslog daemon using the following steps:

1. Check if the Check Point FireWall-1 feature of receiving syslog messages from a remote host is enabled or disabled.
2. If it is disabled, try to enable the feature.
3. Then, try to send any escape sequences through syslog. The following is an example command to perform this action: **echo -e "<189>19: 00:01:04: Test\a\033[2J\033[2;5m\033[1;31mHACKER~ ATTACK\033 [2;25m\033[22;30m\033[3q" | nc -u firewall 514**

Checklist for Secure Log Management

The following is a checklist for maintaining the security of log management:

- Maintain backups of log files.
- Use updated versions of software for logging mechanisms.

- Select secure log file locations.
- Encrypt log files in order to secure log information.
- Store log files on a separate secure host to prevent tampering of log files.
- Check whether the log management infrastructure is secure or not.
- Train the personnel responsible for log management.
- Provide limited access to log files.
- Use a secure application to transmit log files from one system to another.
- Check the internal clocks of all systems.

Chapter Summary

- Log files maintain a record of all actions that occur on an organization's systems and networks.
- Logs are used to perform auditing and forensic analysis to investigate malicious activity.
- Limited storage size for log data leads to overwriting old data with new data or interrupted logging.
- Security software logs are logs that provide a record of security events.
- Logs that record all events related to operating systems are operating system logs.
- Organizations use logging data to gain information security with advanced audits and data correlation.
- Most syslog applications use unreliable connectionless UDP to move or rotate log information between hosts.
- Administrators should use updated versions of software for logging mechanisms.
- Administrators should regularly check the internal clock of the system to ensure the proper logging of events.

Chapter 7

File Integrity Checking

Objectives

After completing this chapter, you should be able to:

- Understand file integrity
- Be able to check the integrity of a file
- Understand CRC-based integrity checking
- Understand hash-based integrity checking
- Enumerate tools used for integrity checking

Key Terms

Cyclic redundancy check (CRC)   a method for checking integrity by taking the original binary data and converting it to a polynomial divided by another predetermined polynomial (key); the remainder from the division is the CRC, which is attached to and transmitted with the original message

Hashing   a mathematical procedure that converts a large variable string of data into a small fixed-size integer that is used to verify the integrity of the original data

Introduction to File Integrity Checking

File integrity checking is an important task, because it allows an individual to check if a file has been corrupted or modified. Files can be corrupted through errors, malicious actions, or hardware faults, and being able to verify the integrity of a file is a valuable skill. This chapter teaches you about file integrity and how to verify it. It also lists tools you can use to check file integrity.

File Integrity Overview

File integrity checking verifies the following:

- If the file is the same as the original file (size and version of the file)
- When the file was last created or modified

- Login name of the user who last modified the file
- The file's attributes (e.g., read only, hidden, system)

File integrity can be compromised due to the following:

- *Faulty storage media*: Files stored on faulty storage media get corrupted and cannot be opened.
- *Transmission errors*: Transmission errors cause damage to a file when it is transmitted from one system to another on the network.
- *Errors during copying or moving*: Errors when a file is copied or moved onto another system may lead to file corruption.
- *Software bugs and viruses*: Malicious programs and software bugs can damage files.

Integrity-Checking Techniques

The following are three common integrity-checking techniques:

1. *Comparing two files bit-by-bit*: Comparing two files bit-by-bit requires both the original copy of the file and the copy that is being checked. These two files are compared bit-by-bit, which is a difficult and time-consuming task and not frequently used.

2. *CRC-based integrity checking*: **Cyclic redundancy check (CRC)** is a method for checking integrity by taking the original binary data and converting it to a polynomial divided by another predetermined polynomial (key). The remainder from the division is the CRC, which is attached to and transmitted with the original message. CRC generates a 32-bit number (CRC value) that depends on the contents of the file. If the file contents change, the CRC value of the file also changes; therefore, the user knows that the file has been modified. It takes input of any length and produces a fixed-sized output. CRC is used for detecting common errors caused by noise in transmission channels by comparing the current version of the file's CRC value with a previously calculated CRC value.

3. *Hash-based integrity checking*: **Hashing** is a mathematical procedure that converts a large variable string of data into a small fixed-size integer that is used to verify the integrity of the original data. Hash-based verification requires a comparison of hash values. In this method, hash algorithms generate a hash value for the file. Hash values of two files can never be the same. This method compares the file's hash value to a previously calculated value to ensure that the file has not been corrupted or modified. If the two hash values match, then it is assumed that the file is the same as the original.

CRC-Based Integrity Checking

The following are the steps for checking a file's integrity with a CRC check:

1. Compute the CRC value of the original file.
2. Compare the CRC value of the current version of the file with the CRC value of the original file.

CRC Checking in Linux

The following are the steps for performing CRC checking on Linux:

1. Change the directory to the folder where the target files are stored.
2. Type **crc32 <original filename>** and press Enter. This displays the CRC of the original file.
3. Type **crc32 <new filename>** and press Enter. This displays the CRC of the current version of the file.
4. Compare the CRC values.
5. To compute the CRC values of all the files in a specific folder, replace the filename with an asterisk (*).

If a file is being transmitted, the sender can compute the CRC value and send that value along with the file. If multiple files are being sent, the sender can create an SFV file, which includes CRC values for all the files being transmitted. This allows the receiver to check the integrity of all the files.

CRC Checking in Windows

The Windows Installer supports CRC checking. After it copies a file, it calculates the CRC of the source and destination files. It then compares the CRC values to make sure they match. If the values do not match, the Windows Installer knows that the file has been modified or corrupted.

Hash-Based Integrity Checking

The following are the steps for hash-based integrity checking:

1. Get the file and previously calculated hash value for the file.
2. Generate a new hash value for the file.
3. Match the old and new hash values.

File Integrity-Checking Tools

The following are file integrity-checking tools:

- cfv
- cksum
- DySFV
- FastSum
- FlashSFV
- FSUM
- HashCalc
- JHashCalc
- Jacksum
- md5sum
- sha1sum
- TeraCopy
- wxChecksums
- SuperSFV
- SFV Checker

Chapter Summary

- File integrity checking verifies if a file is same as the original file and if there have been any modifications made to the file.
- Files stored on faulty storage media get corrupted and cannot be opened.
- Transmission errors cause damage to a file when it is transmitted from one system to another on the network.
- Cyclic redundancy check (CRC) takes an input data stream of any length and produces an output value of a certain fixed size.
- Hash-based verification compares a file's hash value to a previously calculated value for the file to ensure that the file has not been corrupted or modified.
- The Windows Installer supports CRC checking.

Chapter 8

Data Leakage Penetration Testing

Objectives

After completing this chapter, you should be able to:

- Recognize points of data leakage
- Perform data leakage penetration testing
- Use data protection tools

Key Terms

Data leakage an incident in which private and confidential data leak out of an organization's network and into the hands of unauthorized users

Introduction to Data Leakage Penetration Testing

Data leakage is a serious problem, in which private and confidential data leak out of an organization's network and into the hands of unauthorized users. These data could be leaked through e-mail, HTTP, or even a networked printer; a malicious user can do almost anything with these data, especially considering that only about 30% of users encrypt their sensitive data. This chapter teaches you how to perform data leakage penetration testing to protect confidential data from malicious users.

Points of Data Leakage

Data are often leaked through the following points:

- Removable devices, such as those using USB and Firewire
- FTP ports
- Bluetooth
- E-mail attachments
- Memory slots
- Spyware/Trojans

Sensitive Data

Organizations must be sure to take care securing vital and sensitive data, such as the following:

- Employee information such as names, addresses, salaries, and Social Security numbers
- Marketing and new product plans
- Corporate strategies
- Target markets and prospect information
- Business procedures
- Product designs, research, and costs
- Alliance and contract arrangements
- Customer and supplier information
- Credit records or credit union account information
- Trade secrets and intellectual property

Steps for Data Leakage Penetration Testing

The following are the steps for performing data leakage penetration testing.

Step 1: Check the Physical Availability of USB Devices

USB devices are often used for bulk data transfer. Some transfer data inside a system, while others transfer data to outside devices. These devices may be vulnerable to data leakage. Testers need to check the USB devices connected to systems in the Windows Device Manager, shown in Figure 8-1.

Step 2: Check If USB Drives Are Enabled

USB drives directly connect to the computer through USB ports and are mainly used for transferring bulk data. These USB drives only operate if connecting options are enabled, so testers can use the Windows Device Manager to check whether the USB drives are enabled or not, as shown in Figure 8-2.

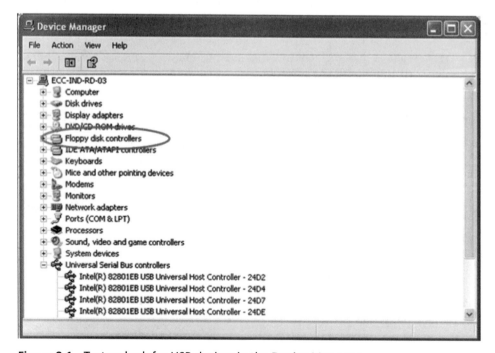

Figure 8-1 Testers look for USB devices in the Device Manager.

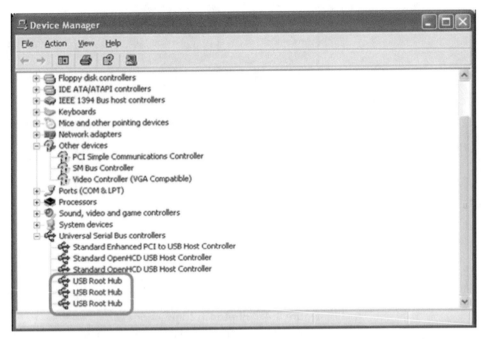

Figure 8-2   These active USB root hubs will connect external USB drives to the system.

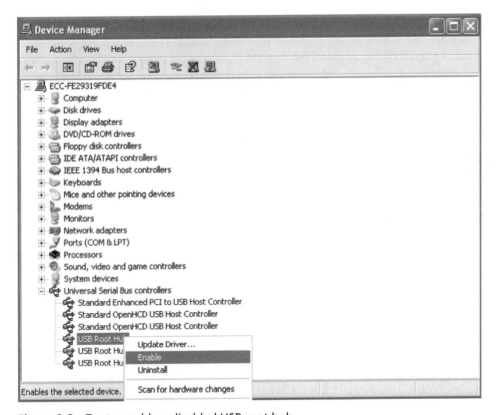

Figure 8-3   Try to enable a disabled USB root hub.

Step 3: Try to Enable USB

If any of the USB root hubs are disabled, indicated by a red X on their icons, testers can try to enable them by right-clicking on one and then clicking **Enable**, as shown in Figure 8-3. If the device then becomes enabled, the active user has administrative privileges, which should not be the case for normal users.

Figure 8-4 Bluetooth connections can allow an attacker to wirelessly steal data.

Step 4: Check If USB Devices Require Passwords

Most USB devices can be secured with a password, which the system will require as soon as the device is connected. Testers can connect the USB devices to the system and check if authentication is requested.

Step 5: Check If Bluetooth Is Enabled

Bluetooth transfers data between systems and wireless devices. Some systems have built-in Bluetooth connections, which could allow attackers to transfer confidential data wirelessly. Penetration testers can use the Windows Device Manager to check if the system has a built-in Bluetooth connection, as shown in Figure 8-4. They can also check if this connection is enabled or disabled. If it is enabled, it should be disabled to protect confidential data. If it is disabled, testers can try to enable it; if it becomes enabled, the current user would have administrative privileges, which should not be the case for normal users.

Step 6: Check If Firewire Is Enabled

Firewire, also known as IEEE 1394, transfers bulk data with speeds of up to 400 Mbps. This speed makes it ideal for external hard drives. Testers can check whether Firewire is enabled or not in the system BIOS.

Step 7: Check If FTP Ports 20 and 21 and/or SSH Port 22 Are Enabled

FTP is used to transfer files from one system to another, usually through ports 20 and 21. Attackers know these are common ports, so testers should check to see if they are enabled in the firewall's configuration. Testers should also check to see if port 22 is enabled. Secure Shell (SSH), even though it is designed to provide confidentiality and integrity of data over an insecure network, still allows for the bulk transfer of information.

Step 8: Check for Available and Enabled Memory Slots

There are many memory slots present on a system, including RAM, SRAM, and virtual memory. These slots store vital information and may be vulnerable to data leakage. Penetration testers should identify all memory resources.

Step 9: Check If Employees Are Using Camera Devices Within Restricted Areas

Employees with camera devices, including digital cameras and most modern mobile phones, can capture confidential data on these devices. Organizations should restrict the use of these devices in sensitive areas to prevent data leakage.

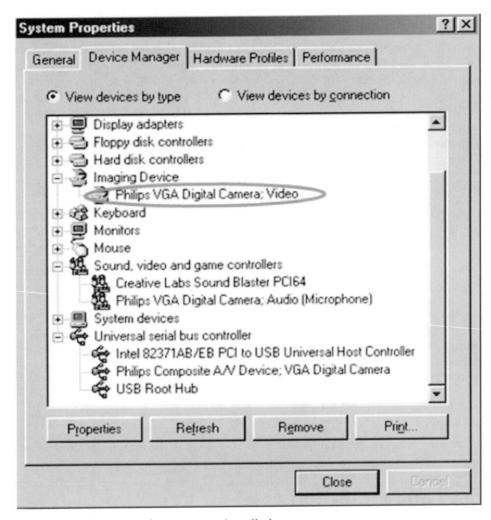

Figure 8-5   This system has a camera installed.

Step 10: Check If Systems Have Camera Drivers

Computer systems can have digital cameras installed. Testers should check if systems have drivers for these cameras in the Windows Device Manager, shown in Figure 8-5.

Step 11: Check for Antispyware and Anti-Trojan Software

Spyware and Trojans can secretly collect sensitive data and send the data to attackers. Penetration testers should check if spyware and Trojans are installed on the system. To check, testers can send a malicious program to the system and see if a defense program stops it.

The following are some popular antispyware software applications:

- Spy Sweeper
- CounterSpy
- Trend Micro Anti-Spyware
- AntiSpy
- Spyware Doctor
- PestPatrol
- Ad-Aware SE/Pro
- Spyware BeGone
- McAfee Anti-Spyware
- Maxion Spy Killer

Step 12: Check Data Encryption Strength

Data encryption techniques protect an organization's vital information from unauthorized users. Various methods can be used to encrypt this data, using translation tables for encryption and decryption. Penetration testers should check the translation table to see if any encryption is used to protect the data.

They should also check for DBMS packets, because many DBMS packets have some kind of encryption scheme. Various key-based encryption algorithms are used to protect vital information, so testers should check which algorithms are being used.

Testers can also apply various data decryption or cryptanalysis tools such as Jipher and Crank on encrypted data. If they can easily decrypt the data, the data are not secure.

Step 13: Check If Internal Hardware Components Are Locked

Many hardware components are present inside systems, such as network adapters and PCMCIA cards. Bulk data are transferred between systems and these devices. Malicious users who have access to the system may use these internal components to gain confidential information, so testers should check whether or not internal hardware components are locked.

Step 14: Check If the Size of E-Mail and E-Mail Attachments Is Restricted

Employees can transfer data outside the network using e-mail attachments. If the size of e-mails and e-mail attachments is restricted, this will be much more difficult. To test this, a penetration tester can try to send an e-mail with a very large attachment to an outside address. If it is sent successfully, it means the size is not restricted.

The following are the steps to check this setting in Microsoft Exchange Server:

1. Open the **Mail Flow Settings** tab in **Mailbox Properties**.

2. Open the **Message Size Restriction** dialog box to see the size limit of sent and received e-mail messages.

3. Click on the option for **Mail Attachment Size** to check the maximum allowed attachment size.

Data Privacy and Protection Acts

The laws in the following sections directly relate to data privacy and protection.

USA: Gramm-Leach-Bliley Act

The Financial Modernization Act of 1999, also known as the Gramm-Leach-Bliley Act or GLB Act, includes provisions to protect consumers' personal financial information held by financial institutions. Section 6801, following, is particularly relevant:[1]

Sec. 6801. Protection of nonpublic personal information

(a) *Privacy obligation policy*

It is the policy of the Congress that each financial institution should have an affirmative and continuing obligation to respect the privacy of its customers and to protect the security and confidentiality of those customers' nonpublic personal information.

(b) *Financial institutions safeguards*

In furtherance of the policy in subsection (a) of this section, each agency or authority described in section 6805(a) of this title shall establish appropriate standards for the financial institutions subject to their jurisdiction relating to administrative, technical, and physical safeguards—

(1) *to insure the security and confidentiality of customer records and information;*

(2) *to protect against any anticipated threats or hazards to the security or integrity of such records; and*

(3) *to protect against unauthorized access to or use of such records or information which could result in substantial harm or inconvenience to any customer.*

USA: Health Insurance Portability and Accountability Act (HIPAA)

The Federal Health Insurance Portability and Accountability Act of 1996, also known as HIPAA, establishes a national framework for security standards and protection of confidentiality in regard to health care data and information.[2]

All health care plans, health care clearinghouses, and health care providers that transmit health information electronically must comply with HIPAA regulations.

USA: The USA PATRIOT Act

The USA PATRIOT Act prescribes penalties for anyone who performs any of these activities:[3]

- Intentionally intercepts, endeavors to intercept, or procures any other person to intercept or endeavor to intercept any wire, oral, or electronic communication
- Intentionally uses, endeavors to use, or procures any other person to use or endeavor to use any electronic, mechanical, or other device to intercept any oral communication
- Intentionally discloses, or endeavors to disclose, to any other person the contents of any wire, oral, or electronic communication, knowing or having reason to know that the information was obtained through the interception of a wire, oral, or electronic communication
- Intentionally uses, or endeavors to use, the contents of any wire, oral, or electronic communication, knowing or having reason to know that the information was obtained through the interception of a wire, oral, or electronic communication

USA: Sarbanes-Oxley Act (SOX)

The Sarbanes-Oxley Act, or SOX, requires companies and registered accounting firms to comply with specific rules regarding the accuracy and reliability of their confidential information.[4] It strengthens the requirements for record maintenance, auditing, and reporting.

UK: Data Protection Act

The Data Protection Act regulates how personal information is used through eight data protection principles.[5] According to the act, personal information must be:

1. Fairly and lawfully processed
2. Processed for limited purposes
3. Adequate, relevant, and not excessive
4. Accurate
5. Not kept longer than necessary
6. Processed in accordance with an individual's rights
7. Kept secure
8. Not transferred abroad without adequate protection

Data Protection Tools

VIP Privacy

VIP Privacy is a tool that searches and safely cleans up information stored on a system, without deleting private files or changing the contents of documents. It only deletes information collected by applications, without interfering with system and application performance.

VIP Privacy's key features include the following:

- Fully customizable search and clear options for safe removal of private data
- Panic mode for quick and easy one-step data removal

- Easy-to-use scheduler for automatic system cleanup
- Indicator of current privacy level for quick safety evaluation
- Exports results to text files

Data Protection Software

Data Protection Software secures data stored on hard drives and removable media. Its features include the following:

- High-speed data protection mechanism
- Creates any number of protected disk images
- Simultaneously connects up to eight protected disks
- Quickly changes the disk access password
- Supports various file systems, including FAT, FAT32, and NTFS
- Quickly mounts frequently used disks
- Quickly deletes protected disks without the possibility of restoration
- Allows for the emergency mounting of used protected disks

FolderAccess

FolderAccess locks files and folders with a personal password. This effectively protects files and folders from malicious programs, including viruses, worms, and Trojans.

VISOCO Data Protection Master

VISOCO Data Protection Master increases the safety and accessibility of data in a Sybase ASE database. Its advantages include the following:

- Creates and supports a copy of a database in real time
- Quickly switches to the reserve server if the main server fails
- Creates a transactions dump and a database dump for later copying to reserve media
- Restores data to almost any point in time using the dump history and transactions log

CryptEnCrypt

CryptEnCrypt is powerful encryption software. It requires a user-supplied password to decrypt files and allows the user to choose from several encryption algorithms.

Steganos Security Suite

Steganos Security Suite encrypts and hides data in self-decrypting e-mails. It also includes Portable Safe and Internet Trace Destructor featuring XP Privacy, Password Manager, and Data Shredder.

Private InfoKeeper

Private InfoKeeper encrypts entire files to provide a highly encrypted and password-protected environment for sensitive data.

QwikSecure File Protection System

QwikSecure File Protection System hides files and folders safely and securely using encrypted passwords. It supports multiple users and allows each user to protect his or her files and folders using individual passwords, or a single common password can be used for all users on a system, if they prefer. QwikSecure includes a simple interface to guide novice users through the process of hiding and revealing files and folders.

Chapter Summary

- Employee information, such as names, addresses, and Social Security numbers, must be protected.
- Points of data leakage include USB, FTP, Bluetooth, e-mail attachments, Firewire, memory slots, spyware, and Trojans.
- Ports 20 and 21 are commonly used for FTP data transfer, making it wise to block them at the firewall.
- Data can be transferred outside the organization's network using large e-mail attachments.
- Testers should check the physical availability of USB devices.
- Testers should check whether Bluetooth and Firewire are enabled.
- Testers should check whether antispyware and anti-Trojan software are enabled.

Endnotes

[1] http://www.ftc.gov/privacy/glbact/glbsub1.htm
[2] http://www.omh.state.ny.us/omhweb/hipaa/
[3] http://www.usdoj.gov/criminal/cybercrime/18usc2511.htm
[4] http://www.dataprotection.com/regulatory-compliance/sox/
[5] http://www.direct.gov.uk/en/RightsAndResponsibilities/DG_10028507

Index